EARLY MODERN SONNETEERS:
FROM WYATT TO MILTON

'POETRY'

EARLY MODERN SONNETEERS:
FROM WYATT TO MILTON

MICHAEL SPILLER

Northcote House
in association with the
British Council

© Copyright 2001 by Michael Spiller

First published in 2001 by Northcote House Publishers Ltd, Horndon, Tavistock, Devon, PL19 9NQ, United Kingdom.
Tel: +44 (01822) 810066 Fax: +44 (01822) 810034.

British Library Cataloguing in Publication Data
A catalogue record for this book is available from the British Library

ISBN 0-7463-0936-8

Typeset by PDQ Typesetting, Newcastle-under-Lyme
Printed and bound in Great Britain by
The Baskerville Press, Salisbury, Wiltshire, SP2 7QB

to Patrick Christie
'an other selfe'

Contents

Biographical Outlines

Alighieri, Dante. Dante was born in Florence in 1265, and died in Ravenna in 1321. (The reader will note that, in common with many early Italian artists, such as Michelangelo and Raphael, Dante is known by his forename, not his family name.) He met Beatrice Portinari first in 1274, and wrote his *Vita nuova* shortly after her death in 1290. Exiled from his native city in 1302 for political offences, he travelled around north Italy, and possibly visited Paris. He lived latterly in Verona until 1319, and is buried in Ravenna. His great epic work (though he did not think of it as an epic, and he did not call it by its now universal title, *The Divine Comedy*) was written between 1300 and 1320.

Petrarch, Francis. Francesco Petrarca was born in Arezzo in 1304, and died at Arquà, in northern Italy, in 1374. His family moved about 1312 to Carpentras, near the cosmopolitan centre of Avignon, in Provence, and he studied law at Montpellier and Bologna. His exceptional scholarly abilities earned him patronage that gave him independence and financial security from 1330 onwards. In 1353 he moved to Italy, and remained in the north of Italy until his death. His reputation as a poet, scholar, humanist, and philosopher was enormously high in his own day, partly because of his own salesmanship, and he is probably the most influential lyric poet in the whole of West European literature. He wrote his sonnets throughout his life, most of them in praise of Laura, whom he said he first saw in Avignon on 6 April 1327; she died, according to Petrarch, on 6 April 1348, of the Black Death. She has been identified, plausibly, with Laura de Sade, wife of Hugues de Sade, a merchant of Avignon. It is not known whether she ever met or even saw Petrarch.

Wyatt, Sir Thomas. Born in 1503 on Sir Henry Wyatt's estate of Allington Castle in Kent and educated at Cambridge University, Wyatt became a courtier and diplomat in the service of Henry VIII, travelling in Italy (where he was captured by Spanish troops); France, and Spain. In the touchy and dangerous atmosphere of the court he contrived, like Surrey, to be imprisoned and knighted in the same year, 1536. He was again arrested after his father's death in 1539, but acquitted of treason, and elected an MP and made a vice-admiral. He died of a fever in 1542. His poems were written throughout his life, though most of his sonnets are thought to have been written before 1537, his appointment as Ambassador to Spain.

Surrey, Henry Howard, Earl of. Born about 1517, he inherited the title of Earl of Surrey when his father, Thomas Howard, became Duke of Norfolk in 1524. He was well educated, and read French and Italian as well as Latin and Greek, though probably not very fluently. Because he was a scion of one of the most powerful families in the court, his career was chequered and ultimately tragic: he was knighted in 1536, made Knight of the Garter and also arrested and imprisoned in 1542, and held various military commands. Finally rivalry at court led to his being arrested, with his father, for treason in 1546. The death of Henry VIII saved the father, but not the son: he was executed on 21 January 1547. He wrote a small number of sonnets which achieved prominence through the publication of *Tottel's Miscellany* (1557), and is usually credited with the first effective use of English blank verse, in his translation of Books 2 and 4 of Virgil's *Aeneid* (published 1557). His combination of good intelligence, wild behaviour, political misfortune, and real literary skill is very characteristic of Renaissance court life.

Locke, Anne. Born Anne Vaughan about 1530, she married Henry Locke, a Protestant merchant in the Cheapside district of London. Well educated by her father, Stephen Vaughan, who was both a merchant and a political and religious agent of Thomas Cromwell, and a devout Calvinist under the tutelage of her stepmother, she was John Knox's hostess when he visited London in 1553. As a Protestant dissenter under Mary Tudor (reigned 1553–8), she travelled with two small children and a maid to Geneva to sit at the feet of Calvin, and her sonnet sequence was annexed to a translation of one of his sermons, published in 1560. Widowed in 1571, she married twice again, and published only one more book, a translation of Jean Taffin's *Of the Markes of the Children of God* (1590). She died as Anne Prowse sometime after 1595. Her son, Henry Lok (the usual spelling), was also a sonneteer, voluminous but not very good.

Sidney, Sir Philip. Like Surrey in many ways, and idealized even more by his age, Sidney was born in 1554 at Penshurst Castle in Kent into one of the powerful English aristocratic families. He was educated well, though he did not take his degree at Oxford, and travelled extensively in Europe, learning languages and meeting scholars and political figures (1572–5). Allowing for the social vocabulary of courtesy and flattery, he does seem to have made a profound impression of grace and intelligence wherever he went. With his very talented brother and sister, Robert and Mary Sidney (Countess of Pembroke), he encouraged poets and men and women of letters, including, notably, Edmund Spenser: his prose romance, *Arcadia*, is dedicated to Mary. He was knighted in 1582. Though his literary abilities, both creative and critical, were formidable, he desperately wanted political success: it was his undoing, for, in his capacity as Governor of Flushing (1585), he was wounded at the Battle of Zutphen (22 September 1586), and died of his wounds on 17 October, aged 32. His literary works were published posthumously (*Arcadia*, 1590; *Astrophel and Stella*, 1591; *The Defence of Poesy*, 1595), and were and are some of the most quoted and influential of the English Renaissance.

Daniel, Samuel. Born probably in 1562 in Somerset, England, Daniel was the son of a music master. His brother John, whose surname is usually spelt Danyel, was one of the most famus lutenists and composers of his day. Daniel studied at Oxford, though like Sidney he did not take a degree, and then travelled on diplomatic service in France and Italy, before becoming involved on his return home with the Sidney family as tutor to Mary Sidney's son, William Herbert (thought to be the 'Mr W.H.' of Shakespeare's *Sonnets*). He was a professional writer, encouraged by Lady Pembroke, and in 1607 received a minor court post. He lived in London until after Shakespeare's death, and died in retirement in Somerset in 1619. He wrote poetry both lyrical and narrative, plays, and critical works.

Spenser, Edmund. Born in London probably in 1552 to relatively poor parents, Spenser still received a good education, and took an MA degree at Pembroke College, Cambridge, in 1576. By 1579 he was in London again under the protection of the Sidney family. With encouragement from Sir Philip Sidney, he wrote and published a work that made him famous, the collection of pastorals known as *The Shepherd's Calendar* (1579). In 1580 he was appointed secretary to Arthur, Lord Grey, the new Lord Deputy of Ireland, and remained in Ireland after Grey's departure as a civil servant, receiving the grant of a small castle and estate at Kilcolman in County Cork. Here in the late 1580s he wrote the first three books of *The Faerie Queene*, and with Sir Walter Raleigh's support travelled to London in 1589 to see them published and dedicated to the Queen. He did not, however, receive further preferment, and returned to Ireland, where he married (for the second time) in 1594. He published the second part of his epic in 1596, and lived in Ireland until driven out by Tyrone's insurrection in 1598. The Administration in Ireland sent him to London with dispatches, and he died there suddenly in January 1599. He was buried in Westminster Abbey, an indication of the high reputation he enjoyed among his contemporaries as 'the Virgil of England'.

Drayton, Michael. Born like Shakespeare in Warwickshire, in 1563, Drayton was educated in the household of Sir Henry Goodere. He began writing lyric poetry in the mid-1590s, and moved on, in the hierarchy of Renaissance poetics, to historical narrative. Like Spenser, he designed a very ambitious long poem, a kind of survey of England, called *Polyolbion*, published in two parts in 1612 and 1622. He also wrote pastorals, satires, and plays. Though without Spenser's high reputation, he lived to become a grand old man of Jacobean poetry, and was buried in Westminster Abbey on his death in 1631.

Shakespeare, William. Born in Stratford-on-Avon in April 1564, Shakespeare was the son of a dealer in agricultural produce. He was to follow his father's business, but a liaison with a farmer's daughter produced a marriage and a daughter in 1583, with twins a year later. Shakespeare thereupon left his family to make his way in London, probably about 1585, and joined a company of actors. He wrote plays, narrative poems, and sonnets in the early 1590s, in a way very typical of young poets establishing a reputation, but was so good at playwriting that he did not, like Spenser or Drayton, attempt a major epic or narrative poem. By 1597 he was wealthy enough to obtain a grant of arms for his father and himself, and to purchase a large house in Stratford. He then continued as a London playwright with intermittent visits to Stratford, and retired there in 1611. He died in April 1616, survived by his wife and two daughters. Despite the relatively very large amount of information about Shakespeare's life, there is no record of his opinions of his own work, and nothing suggests that he thought of his plays – or indeed his sonnets – as anything but a means to wealth and a comfortable inheritance for his dependants; he is in that sense at once the greatest and (except perhaps for Locke and Herbert) the least literary figure of all those mentioned here.

Donne, John. Donne was born in 1572 in the heart of the City of London, to a prosperous ironmonger, John, and his wife Elizabeth, daughter of John Heywood the dramatist and poet. The family was Catholic, and Donne was probably privately educated before going to both Oxford and Cambridge universities, though as a Catholic he could not take a degree – after his conversion, he was made MA of Oxford in 1610 and DD at Cambridge in 1615. In 1592 he entered one of the Inns of Court in London, a popular finishing school for young gentlemen. Possibly because his brother Henry was imprisoned, and his mother had moved to Antwerp, on religious grounds, and because as a Catholic he could not enter any kind of public service, Donne converted to Protestantism about 1597, apparently after much theological and historical reading. He obtained a post as secretary to Sir Thomas Egerton, Lord Keeper of the Great Seal of England, but ruined his prospects by marrying, without approval, Anne More, Egerton's niece by marriage. Donne was dismissed in 1601. He and his family lived poorly on small acts of patronage and help until he was persuaded, it is said by King James VI and I, to take holy orders, which he did in 1615. His wife died in 1617, and he developed a preoccupation with mortality and death, becoming one of the most famous preachers of his age. He was appointed Dean of St Pauls Cathedral, London, in 1621, and died in its Deanery in 1631. The split in his life between secular and clerical employment is exactly reflected in his poetry, split between his early 'profane' verses, and his later religious work.

Herbert, George. Born in 1593 in Wales, and brother to the diplomat philosopher Lord Herbert of Cherbury, George Herbert was educated by his pious mother, Magdalene Herbert, and afterwards at Trinity College, Cambridge (MA 1615). He became University Orator (1619–27) and seemed set for court advancement; but the death of the King in 1625, and the deaths of other powerful friends, made him decide to take holy orders. He was given the rectory of Bemerton by the Earl of Pembroke, and became the very type of the ideal parish priest. Weakened by lung disease, he died in 1633, and his poems were published posthumously – the music that he is known to have composed for the lute has not survived.

Wroth, Lady Mary (née Sidney). Born in 1586 or 1587, the daughter of Sir Philip Sidney's brother Robert, himself a competent sonnet-writer, she married Sir Robert Wroth in 1604, and seems to have begun writing poetry about 1610. Sir Robert died in 1614, leaving her considerably in debt. With a reputation both as a writer and as a patroness of writers, she was one of the literary foci of southern England, and knew Chapman, Jonson, Wither, Donne, Drummond of Hawthornden, and many others. Her prose romance, *The Countess of Montgomery's Urania* (1621), with its attendant sonnet sequence, *Pamphilia to Amphilanthus*, was widely thought to be a covert description of her own circle of acquaintances, though no key to it has been found. Amphilanthus (the 'double forsaker') is thought to stand for William Herbert, the supposed dedicatee of Shakespeare's *Sonnets*, who became her lover after her husband's death, and had two illegitimate children by her. She died around 1651.

Drummond of Hawthornden, William. Born in 1585 near Edinburgh as the eldest son of a knight with a small estate, Drummond was educated at what is now Edinburgh University with a view to a legal career, and travelled to Paris and Bourges for study. On his father's early death in 1610 he settled on his estate of Hawthornden outside Edinburgh, and lived there, with few absences, for the rest of his life. He had an extremely good private library, with a strong emphasis upon European poetry, and published his first volume of poems in 1616. He was visited at Hawthornden by Ben Jonson in 1618, and corresponded with Michael Drayton. His second volume, mainly of religious poems, *Flowers of Sion*, appeared in 1623. He wrote the script of a pageant for the entry of King Charles into Edinburgh in 1633, and thereafter devoted himself mainly to political pamphleteering and historiography. By judiciously keeping his head down, he avoided persecution during the Civil Wars, and died peacefully in 1649. The title 'of Hawthornden' is conventionally kept with Drummond's name to distinguish him from several other William Drummonds active in Scotland in his lifetime.

Milton, John. Born in 1608 in Bread Street, City of London, the birthplace also of John Donne, Milton was descended from an Oxfordshire Catholic family: his father became a Protestant, and earned his living as a scrivener, a professional writer of legal and contractual documents. Milton was at first privately educated, unusually by a Scots Presbyterian, Thomas Young, and afterwards at Christ's College, Cambridge. From 1632 to 1638 he lived with his father (from whom he had his love and knowledge of music), now retired to the country, and read and studied to become a poet, producing *L'Allegro, Il Penseroso, Arcades, Comus, and Lycidas.* His father was wealthy enough to allow Milton then to travel in France and Italy, as far south as Naples. On his return he married, rather hastily and not altogether happily, and devoted himself to pamphlet writing, mainly against episcopacy. In the year of the execution of Charles I, 1649, he was appointed Latin Secretary to the Council of State, roughly equivalent to today's British Cabinet. By 1652 he had become permanently blind, but continued to write and publish. He was now widowed, and in 1656 married the woman whose death following a stillbirth in 1658 occasioned his last sonnet – Catherine Woodcock, the subject of 'Methought I saw my late espoused Saint'. At the restoration of Charles II, in 1660, he was in considerable danger, but his physical helplessness and the intercession of friends and admirers saved him. *Paradise Lost* was written between 1658 and the year of its publication, 1664, and after that came *Paradise Regained* and *Samson Agonistes* (1671). Milton continued to write voluminously in prose also, but it was his epic verse that established him as one of the leading poets of an age that was by now antipathetic to almost all he believed in. Living quietly in London, he became something of a tourist attraction, and died peacefully at his home in Bunhill Fields in 1674.

Introduction

As we go into a new millennium, one of Britain's major publishing houses has produced a very lively anthology of sonnets, *101 Sonnets from Shakespeare to Heaney*.[1] This vote of confidence in the continuing popularity of sonnets has a quirky but informative introduction, in which the editor, casting a wary eye on people like me, declares that 'one of the most amusing things about all the po-faced or bloody asseverations on what constitutes the "true" sonnet is that no one can agree on anything but the fact that it has fourteen lines.'[2] Unfortunately, not even that: George Meredith and Tony Harrison have written sonnets with sixteen lines, John Donne wrote one with eighteen, and John Milton one with twenty lines. But there were norms of sonnet writing, which this book will describe, and to which most of the writers we shall mention adhered. Everyone who wrote sonnets knew other sonnets, probably in a few different languages: this little block of fourteen lines (or so) was a huge international enterprise, and even now as I write this, and you read it, somebody somewhere in the world is writing yet another sonnet, thank goodness.

To be a sonneteer, whether early and modern or not, is a different kind of activity from being a dramatist, or a novelist, or even an epic poet. The drama, the novel, and the epic are all literary forms, or genres, that demand a sustained commitment, and frequently, indeed, provide the livelihood of the writer; the sonnet, by contrast, is an extremely small literary form, and the reader of this book may well be wondering what it is about the sonnet that causes a substantial number of writers who used it to appear as the subjects of a volume in this series.

As a brief answer, which the rest of this book will expand on, it can be said that the fourteen-line sonnet is the longest lived of

1

all European short verse forms: it has been used by poets ever since its invention about AD 1235, and is still being employed in languages as diverse as Russian and Mandarin today. Most major European and American poets have attempted to write sonnets, and many have written really substantial numbers of them: Ronsard, Tasso, Wordsworth, Berryman, for example. Early in the sonnet's development, it was discovered that separate sonnets could be linked in a curious kind of half-narrative, called a sonnet sequence, and many great literary figures have produced major works in this form: Dante, Petrarch, Sir Philip Sidney, Shakespeare, Rilke, for example. Thus the sheer quantity and quality of sonnet writing forces this apparently minor form into prominence.

Historically and with respect to sonnets written in English, one notices that there are two periods of sonnet production that are remarkable both for quantity and for quality: the nineteenth century in Britain and America, and the period 1580–1620 in Britain. In looking at this latter period, we need to consider both the precursors of the sonnet vogue, such as Sir Thomas Wyatt, writing about 1525–30, and also the aftermath in the seventeenth century, simply because John Milton chose to write a small number of sonnets that rank among the best in our literature; thus the period from 1525 to the last years of Milton, about 1670, is the concern of this volume. At its centre, as it were, are the sonnets of Shakespeare, remarkable enough in themselves, but of course gaining immensely in interest because of what they apparently express of the otherwise quite unknown inner life of our greatest dramatist.

Sonnet writing is also cumulative: anyone who writes a sonnet (after the very first sonnets of all) knows what a sonnet is before the pen hits the paper, and what he or she knows it to be is the sum total of the sonnets he or she has read. In our period, British writers were aware of sonnet writing in both Italian and French, sometimes at first hand, sometimes in translation or adaptation, as well as of the sonnets of their predecessors in English. They had in their minds before they began to write a repertoire of sonnet forms, variations associated with this or that writer; and a treasury of themes and motifs, again associated with particular writers or movements. One particular writer, the Italian Francis Petrarch (1304–74 – see below) almost single-handedly supplied the whole of Renaissance Europe with the themes and motifs of love poetry, and, as he happened to choose the sonnet himself, his prestige attached to the sonnet form as well, and no later sonnet-writer could fail to be influenced either by Petrarch himself (Petrarchan writing) or by his imitators (Petrarchist writing). This holds true for both a writer such as William Drummond of Hawthornden (1585–1649), almost all of whose sonnets contain material borrowed from others, and William Shakespeare, whose sonnets seem to contain no borrowings whatsoever, and it is true of writers in languages other than English – the sonnet was a European form in the Renaissance, and is now a worldwide one.

There was a good deal of argument among critics and practitioners of the sonnet in the sixteenth and seventeen centuries about whether the sonnet could in only fourteen lines say anything very serious or sublime; but the existence of many sonnet sequences and the persistent attention given to the sonnet by literary artists such as Tasso, Ronsard, Donne, and Shakespeare gives an empirical answer that most readers will be happy with.

Exactly why so many writers favoured the sonnet rather than some similar short verse form is unprovable, since poets in our period did not often provide explanations of their own poetry; Petrarch's dominance is one reason, and such comments as we have suggest that the sonnet was considered a challenging form: long enough to allow serious attention to a subject, but short enough to demand conciseness, wit, and a certain epigrammatic definiteness. John Donne said that he would 'build in sonnets pretty rooms' (in 'The Canonization'); Gabriele d'Annunzio said that writing a sonnet made him feel like Benvenuto Cellini working in gold, and Wordsworth famously compared Milton's sonnets to trumpet calls: short, but piercing, clear and soul stirring. Any poet who thought of writing more than occasional sonnets knew that the most famous love poet of Western Europe, Petrarch, had celebrated his mistress in a sonnet *sequence,* and was encouraged by the taste of the age to do likewise. In this challenge of the form there is also the pleasure of game playing: the sonnet has generated all sorts of intricate variations, many designed to do no more than make completion more difficult. Something between a trumpet call and a

3

crossword, then, is this little form and its developed variants, and, if we politely ignore the eighteenth century, practically every major poet in European literature has thought it worth his or her attention at least once or twice.

Before we consider the achievements of particular writers in English between 1525 and 1670, the reader needs to have an outline of the creation and development of the sonnet, since in a way the British came very late to the form, which had been running for some three centuries before Sir Thomas Wyatt wrote the first sonnets in English. The next section will, therefore, give a brief history of the sonnet up to its arrival in Britain, with an emphasis on those features of it that were to turn out to be particularly relevant to English literature.

1

The Invention
of the Sonnet

From the start, the sonnet has had fourteen lines arranged in two groups, of eight and six lines in that order. The eight-line group is known as the *octave*, and it usually divides into two *quatrains*, the second quatrain repeating the rhymes of the first, thus: ABAB ABAB or ABBA ABBA. The six-line group is known as the *sestet*, and it usually divides either into two groups of three, called *tercets*, rhyming CDC DCD or CDE CDE (in Italy), or into one quatrain and a couplet (Britain) rhyming CDCD EE. British writers also favoured an octave in which the rhymes of the second quatrain changed: ABAB CDCD (less commonly, ABBA CDDC). Typically an early Italian sonnet runs: ABBA ABBA CDE CDE, and a British one ABAB CDCD EFEF GG. There is a distinctive French sonnet form, ABBA ABBA CC DEDE (or DEED), which was hardly ever used by British writers, though both French and British writers used the Italian form, particularly in the nineteenth century.

Since the sonnet is not fundamentally symmetrical (8/6) early writers felt the need for some kind of progression or alteration at the end of the octave, and called this point in the sonnet the 'turn', or *volta* in Italian. However, each of the asymmetrical parts is itself symmetrical: 4/4 and then 3/3. In British writing, symmetry becomes repetition, as 4/4:3/3 gives way to 4/4/4:2, and the balance of forces in the British sonnet is really very different from that in the Italian or French, though the idea that some sort of a change should occur after line 8 was common to all. The Italian poets, who had the sonnet to themselves until about 1520, invented various kinds of extension of the sonnet.

'Tailed sonnets', which have a half-line after the fourteenth, and then two more full length lines, and another two and a half, if you want, were popular for comic and satirical purposes, and Milton wrote one when he was feeling cross with his religious opponents, 'On the New Forcers of Conscience'; it rhymes ABBA ABBA CDE DEC c FF f GG. The 'doubled sonnet' in which half-lines were added throughout in various positions (e.g. AaBBbA AaBBbA CDdE DEeC) was also much used in Italy. There were also contracted sonnets, with lines of only six or eight syllables. What never disappears, however, in all these variations, is the basic 8 + 6 structure – even a sonnet of twenty-one lines, 8 + 4: 6 + 3, still respects it. In modern times, unrhymed sonnets exist, and also, in the poetry of George Meredith and Tony Harrison most notably, the sixteen-line sonnet. Here one simply has to judge – both poet and reader – whether a sonnet rhyming ABAB CDCD EFEF GHGH, for example, has the kind of structure that leads one to read the last four lines as a simple expansion of a final couplet (GG) or not. It is the asymmetrical 8 + 6 structuring of thought, rhymes, syntax, and metre that is at the heart of the sonnet's identity, and a poem that has that is a sonnet; a poem that does not, even if it is in fourteen lines, is not a sonnet, or is perhaps a very bad one. For the purposes of this book, as the writers discussed used the 'normal' sonnet almost exclusively, we shall not be dealing with sonnet variants.

All this, of course, exists as a kind of potential in the air before the writer decides what he or she is actually going to say. The sonnet is the bicycle of literature: a design so perfectly adapted to the human frame that it has never been fundamentally changed since its invention, though all sorts of variations and improvements have been made: and before you get on it, you know how you will have to balance and steer, even before you decide where you will go. Admirably suited to short journeys, it will take you on very much longer ones if you have the stamina.

The inventor of this fourteen-line literary transport is a shadowy figure, a lawyer in the south of Italy in the early thirteenth century named Giacomo da Lentino – the surname, as often at that time, identifies the town from which the family comes, in this case, Lentino in eastern Sicily. At that time, the courts and noble households of France, Provence, and north

Italy encouraged poetry in their vernaculars, practised profes-
sionally by the trouvères or troubadours, and casually by
educated men and women. In that cultural climate, it is not
surprising to find a group of educated courtiers around the
Emperor Frederick II (ruled 1208–50) playing with light verse in
their Sicilian dialect of Italian. We have no contemporary
manuscripts, but anthologies compiled at the end of the
thirteenth century give us thirty-five sonnets from this circle,
twenty-five of which are credited to Giacomo da Lentino. He left
no comments on his poetry, not even in the poetry itself, and its
dating is uncertain, but it seems reasonable to think that it was
he who invented the sonnet about the year 1235, and that his
acquaintances at the court of Frederick II liked it and took it up.

If he experimented, we have no trace of it; there are no
almost-sonnets or imperfect ones in the collections. He seems to
have got it right first time: fourteen lines rhyming ABAB ABAB
CDE CDE (fifteen sonnets) and ten rhyming ABAB ABAB CCD
CCD. The lines are eleven syllables long, a length that also
became a European standard. The length of line is of course
independent of the rhyme scheme – a sonnet can have only one
syllable to a line, or many more than eleven – but for reasons
that are still obscure, and have nothing to do with the
development of the sonnet itself, the ten-syllable line, which
becomes an eleven-syllable line in Italian, was establishing itself
in France and Italy as a workhorse line for longer poems, and
was to become the standard blank-verse line of European poetry
everywhere. The best structural explanation that can be given
for its success is that ten or eleven syllables seems to be about
right, in the main European languages, for 'making a point';
indeed, in early poetry the ten/eleven syllable line was known as
a *punto*, and often carried a punctuation mark at the end of it
because it in some way made a complete statement. Whatever
the reasons, da Lentino chose it, and was as lucky with posterity
in that, as in the sonnet's other features. 140–54 syllables seems
to offer a very satisfying amount of space for lyric utterance,
long enough to allow development of an idea in at least two
parts (8/6), and short enough to demand wit and conciseness in
its completion.

Here is one of da Lentino's sonnets, showing how all these
features come together. Punctuation is modern, and the main

7

verbs are underlined, so that the reader not familiar with Italian can form an idea of how the clause and sentence structure coincides with the lines.

> Lo basilisco a lo speclo lucente
>   traggi a morire con isbaldimento;
> lo cesne canta plu gioiosamente
>   quand' è plu presso a lo suo finimento;
> lo paon turba, istando plu gaudente,
>   poi ch' a suoi piedi fa riguardamento;
> l'augel fenise s'arde veramente,
>   per ritornare i' novo nascimento.
> In ta' nature eo sentom' abenuto,
>   ch'allegro vado a morte, a le belleze,
>   e 'nforzo il canto presso a lo finire;
> estando gaio torno dismaruto;
>   ardendo in foco inovo in allegreze,
>   per voi, plu gente, a cui spero redire.

[The basilisk is drawn rejoicing to its death in the polished mirror; the swan sings most joyfully when nearest to its end; the peacock is perturbed, just at its most joyful, when it beholds its feet; the phoenix really burns in order to return in a new birth.

These natures I feel I have adopted, for I go joyfully to my death, towards beauty, and I urge my song when near my end; being joyful, I change to dismay; burning in fire, I am reborn in joy, because of you, noble lady, to whom I hope to return.]

One can see that da Lentino is thinking through the pattern as it is described above: in the octave, he allots two lines in the quatrains to each animal: the basilisk (whose glance was said to kill, and which could thus be killed by facing it with a mirror); the swan, the peacock, and the phoenix. At the sestet, he 'turns' all this, using the collective adjective *tai* ('such'), to apply to himself, but getting four animals into six lines is slightly more complicated: two general points ('These natures I feel I have adopted...because of you, noble lady, to whom I hope to return') frame four lines each containing the human application of one animal. Each line except the first contains a verb, and thus makes a point, though not necessarily a self-contained one. The combination of iteration (lines 1–8), summary (line 9), parallelism (lines 10–13), and climax (line 14) is really very satisfying, even at the distance of seven and a half centuries.

If the reader will allow me to move at this point from the

8

bicycle to the games board, what da Lentino has done is to create a frame, or board, which imposes certain arbitrary but pleasing rules on the player, who must complete certain patterns but has an infinite number of ways to do it And, as the sonnet went down the centuries, players discovered that they could refuse certain patterns – like, for example, the turn at the ninth line – but that to do so was of course to draw attention to the pattern by avoiding or altering it: in the sixteenth century, some Italian sonneteers began to run the eighth line on into the ninth, postponing the 'turn', and this was a subtlety particularly appreciated because it drew attention to itself by countering expectation. When at a later point in this book we come to the question of what makes a 'good' sonnet, the reader may care to recall the board-game analogy, and reflect on what it is that makes one say, 'That was a *good* game!'

The surviving sonnets from da Lentino's time show a number of question-and-answer groups: one member of the circle would write a sonnet asking, say, 'What is true devotion?', and friends would reply in sonnet form using the same rhymes, making a set of sonnets that is known as a *tenzone*. Thus early, then, we have not only the structure and dynamics of the individual sonnet but also the idea that sonnets can be connected up. Very quickly the successors of the Sicilian poets at Frederick's court, the poets of the northern Italian city states in the later thirteenth century, produced *sonnet sequences*. No rules emerged to control the length of these, and the custom was to key the number of sonnets to some set of objects like the seven deadly sins (Guittone d'Arezzo, about 1260) or the months of the year (Folgore da San Gemignano, *c*.1310). The sonnet thus became a means of dealing with, or responding to, the discrete identity of things and also their interconnections – though that is a very modern way of explaining what these writers would have thought of as a rhetorical exercise in exposition of a topic.

2

Dante Alighieri
(1265–1321)

One writer who did, however, have a sense of the sonnet as an existential space was Dante Alighieri. Dante's mind was so energetic, and his personality so extraordinary, that whatever literary form he selected became remarkable in his hands – *terza rima* for his *Divine Comedy*, and, for our purposes, the sonnet for his autobiographical work, *La Vita nuova*, 'The New Life'. Composed about 1292, the book is a chain of twenty-six sonnets and five other poems embedded in a prose narrative telling the story of his encountering and falling in love with Beatrice, the girl who was to become, after her death in 1291, the tutelary saint of the *Divine Comedy*.

Each sonnet reflects upon a quality or attribute of Beatrice as it affects her lover, sometimes linked to a specific incident, a look or an encounter or a remark. It moves characteristically from the girl, or from something connected to her, to the reaction of Dante himself, perplexed, grief-stricken, overcome, baffled, elevated; and the prose narrative round about then inserts this emotional epiphany back into a kind of chronological account anchored in the Florence of Dante's own youth.The sonnets are at once less expository and more egocentric than those of Giacomo da Lentino, and show the first close link between the sonnet form and what the writers of Elizabethan England would call 'the passionate mind' – that is, the mind disordered by its emotions ('passions'):

> 'L'amaro lagrimar che voi faceste,
>   oi occhi miei, così lunga stagione,
>   facea lagrimar l'altre persone

10

de la pietate, come voi vedeste.
Ora mi par che voi l'obliereste,
   s'io fosse dal mio parte sì fellone
   ch'i' non ven disturbasse ogne cagione,
membrandovi colei cui voi piangeste.
  La vostra vanità mi fa pensare
    e spaventami sì, ch'io temo forte
     del viso d'una donna che vi mira.
   Voi non dovreste mai, se non per morte,
  la vostra donna, ch'è morta, obliare.'
   Cosi dice 'l meo core, e poi sospira.

(Vita nuova, 37)

['The bitter tears you used to shed, my eyes, for so long a time, made other people weep from pity, as you saw. Now it seems to me that you would forget her, if I for my part were so treacherous as not to bring every reason before you, reminding you of her for whom you lament.

Your shallowness makes me wonder, and frightens me so that I really fear the sight of any lady who looks on you. You should never, until death itself, forget your Lady who is dead.' So speaks my heart, and then sighs.]

This elaborate dramatizing of internal anguish is at once formal – the heart makes a speech to the eyes – and highly passionate. Dante was not alone in this: he was a member of quite a large circle of poets known collectively as the *stilnovisti* ('the new stylists'), who all wrote sonnets and other poems in this manner; but he uniquely provided a sonnet sequence using the sonnet for glimpses of intense moments in a psychological development.

11

3

Francis Petrarch
(1304–1374)

Dante Alighieri died in 1321, and the fame of his *Divine Comedy* eclipsed that of the *Vita nuova*, whose sonnets were not especially well known in Britain until the nineteenth century. But his idea that the sonnet could be used for what we might loosely call emotional autobiography was picked up by the poet who became the great master of all Renaissance sonneteering, Francis Petrarch (Francesco Petrarca), born in Arezzo near Florence in 1304.

Whether directly because he had read Dante's work, or indirectly through a general acquaintance with the poetry of his time, which he read in Latin, Italian, and Provençal, Petrarch began about 1330 to write sonnets about his own Beatrice, a woman named Laura, whom, he declared, he first saw at matins in the Church of St Clare in Avignon on 6 April 1327, and loved for the rest of his life (he died in 1374, sitting at his desk in his high house in Arquà in the Eugenaean Hills of north Italy). She is thought to have been Laura de Sade, wife of a merchant in Avignon; she probably never talked to nor even met Petrarch, and she died in the Black Death that ravaged Europe in 1348.

However fictional or idealized, Petrarch's adoration of Laura was constant, and produced by the end of his life a collection of 366 poems about her and his life in relation to her, 317 of which are sonnets. We know that they are a collection, not just because he left a very carefully prepared manuscript of them but because he said so, in a sonnet written about 1350 that now stands as the prefatory sonnet of his *Rime sparse* ('Scattered Verses' – the title is from the prefatory sonnet itself):

Voi ch'ascoltate in rime sparse il suono	A	
di quei sospiri ond'io nudriva 'l core	B	first quatrain
in sul mio primo giovenil errore	B	
quand' era in parte altr'uom da quel ch'i' sono:	A	
del vario stile in ch'io piango e ragiono	A	
fra le vane speranze e 'l van dolore	B	second quatrain
ove sia chi per prova intenda amore	B	
spero trovar pietà, non che perdono.	A	[volta: 'turn']
Ma ben veggio or sì come al popol tutto	C	
favola fui gran tempo, onde sovente	D	first tercet
di me medesmo meco mi vergogno;	E	
e del mio vaneggiar vergogna è 'l frutto	C	
e 'l pentersi, e 'l conoscer chiaramente	D	second tercet
che quanto piace al mondo è breve sogno.	E	

[You who listen, in these scattered poems, to the sound of the sighs with which I fed my heart during the first errors of my youth, when I was in part another person from what I am now; for the different styles in which I weep and argue between vain hope and vain grief, where there is anyone who from experience understands love, I hope to find pity, if not pardon.

But I now see clearly how for long I was the talk of the crowd, for which often within myself I am ashamed of my very self; and of my extravagance, shame is the fruit, and repentance, and the clear knowledge that whatever pleases the world is a brief dream.]

If Petrarch had known that his *Rime sparse* was to become the Bible of European love poetry two and three hundred years later – which would have pleased him enormously, since he was a persistent and successful salesman of his own talents – he might have thought of this sonnet as a manifesto of the Petrarchan self, an 'I' very prominent in this sonnet, and marked by violently contrasting states of feeling. We are apt to think of interest in the instability of the self and the problems of uttering it as certainly post-Cartesian and probably post-Freudian: but Petrarch knew the *Confessions* of St Augustine and possibly Dante's *Vita nuova* as well as the autobiographical writings of Cicero, Seneca, and Pliny, and had a model, or models, of the self not very distant from our own existential frame of reference. Since he became so important to later sonneteers, we need a brief explanation of this self-fashioning here.

The idea that each person has a *self*, a collection of attributes attached and attachable to their personal name, is implicit in the earliest inscriptions that say, in effect, 'My name is Ozymandias,

King of Kings...', but the idea that people can write about themselves comes rather later, and brings with it the idea of the divided self: plainly the person who writes now is in some sense the same as, but also in some senses different from, the person who was then: the present, writing self has the power to make an account and an accounting (the pun is a very fertile one) of the past self. Of the many ways in which this can be done, one emerges in Western Europe in the late Middle Ages as particularly relevant to the sonnet: the confession. Following the model of St Augustine's *Confessions* and the confessional practice of the Catholic Church, it became common for individuals (that is, people aware that what attached to their personal names was different from what attached to others') to review what they had been and assess it, either in an approving way ('Log Cabin to White House') or a cautionary way (Petrarch, as above).

Now a single sonnet is not long enough to tell a story, but, as Dante discovered, a number of sonnets each of which recounts a moment of experience can be assembled into a kind of story of the self. In the sonnet quoted above, written by Petrarch somewhere about 1350, the confessional principle of self-organization is attached clearly (and prestigiously, given Petrarch's later fame) to the sonnet sequence, and no one thereafter writing sonnets in any language in Europe could be unaware of it (though they did not have to assemble their own sonnets at all, and many collections exist in quite miscellaneous form).

Within the framework of a sonnet sequence thus oriented towards some kind of accounting of the self ('Read here, sweet maid, the story of my woes'; 'How do I love thee? let me count the ways'), each sonnet tends naturally to become the record of a moment of suffering, and it was again Petrarch who gave to European poetry the semiotic manifestation of suffering (usually suffering for love) – antithesis. Deeply rooted in the Christian humanist tradition, and with earlier precedent in Platonism, the antitheses between contrary states of the human soul or mind were seen as the markers of self-knowledge, and the intensity with which these contrary states were experienced became the intensity of life itself for the Petrarchan lover. Sonnets that dealt with the love of God rather than secular love could equally use this sense of the 'I' as a locus of conflict between opposites, a view congenial to Calvinism particularly: and thus the Petrarchan semiotics of the self, associated continually with the sonnet form, became for some two or three hundred years the most popular expressive vocabulary in European literature. When Cherubino, in Mozart's *Marriage of Figaro* (1786), declares in adolescent anguish, 'Non so più cosa son, cosa faccio', ('I don't know what I am or what I'm doing any longer'), it is for Petrarchan imagery that he reaches to explain himself – comic, but still comprehensible after four centuries.

4

Sir Thomas Wyatt
(1503?–1542)

What this meant for later writers, and particularly for the British
writers with whom we are mainly concerned, may be illustrated
by one of Sir Thomas Wyatt's sonnets, as we now turn to his
introduction of the sonnet into English literature:

> If waker care, if sodayne pale colour,
>   If many sighes with litle speche to playne,
>   Now joy, now woe, if they my chere distayne
> For hope of smalle, if much to fere therefore,
> To hast, to slak my pase lesse or more,
>   Be signe of love, then do I love agayne;
>   If thow aske whome, sure sins I did refrayne
> Brunet, that set my welth in such a rore,
> Th'unfayned chere of Phillis hath the place
>   That Brunet had: she hath and ever shal.
>   She from myself now hath me in her grace:
> She hath in hand my wit, my will and all;
>   My hert alone wel worthie she doth staye,
>   Without whose helpe skant do I live a daye.

playne: complain; *my chere distayne*: disfigure my looks; *slak my pase*: slow my
pace; *sins*: since; *rore*: uproar, confusion; *unfayned chere*: sincere behaviour;
staye: support, stabilize

Wyatt must have had in memory or in front of him a sonnet
by Petrarch, *Rime*, 224, which begins in the same way: 'S'una
fede amorosa, un cor non finto, un languir dolce, un desiar
cortese...' ['If a loving devotion, an unfeigning heart, a sweet
languishing, a courteous desire...']; he had translated this once,
but what he now produces is not a translation or even an
adaptation, but a fresh response to a Petrarchan cue: what are

16

the marks of the lover? With a fair degree of whimsicality (Phyllis is unlikely to last much longer than Brunette, one feels), Wyatt sketches a persona marked by extremes: too much of one thing, too little of another, now in joy, now in woe, at odds with himself, in love and at risk of death. This unfixed, vibrating mode of existence in verse probably had very little to do with the business of real life, as Henry VIII's unfortunate queens no doubt realized at the last, but it was to prove enduringly popular in Britain, and indeed all over Europe, in the sixteenth century.

The story of the revival of interest in Petrarch by a skilled publicist and disciple, Pietro Bembo (1470–1547) is too long for insertion here.[1] What it meant was that for anyone living, like Wyatt, in or around a Renaissance court in the sixteenth century, when Italian art, literature, and music were the desirable standard of fashion, Petrarch's love poetry was the summit of poetic art in one's vernacular. Renaissance princes both inside and outside Italy were much occupied with acquiring prestige and giving patronage, and Petrarchan verse writing became intensely fashionable for courtiers, which in turn meant that the sonnet became a much practised form. The people most likely to encounter Petrarchan or Petrarchist verse were diplomats and merchants, those whose professions gave them a working knowledge of foreign languages, not of course taught in the educational system of the day, and their occupations also brought them into contact with the sophisticated urban classes of other countries.

Exactly this seems to have happened to Thomas Wyatt (later Sir Thomas), who travelled abroad as a minor diplomat for his king, Henry VIII, and in 1526 visited the French court of Francis I, where French poets were spreading the knowledge of Petrarch and Petrarchism. In the following year, he went to Rome; his capture by Spanish troops is unlikely to have introduced him to Spanish Petrarchism, but in 1537 he became the King's ambassador to Spain, and travelled there via one of the great French cultural centres, Lyons. He would therefore have had a working knowledge of French, Italian, and (rather later) Spanish at a time when all three countries were publishing sonnets in their vernaculars in imitation of Petrarch, and he may even have met the French and Spanish pioneers of the sonnet, Clément Marot (1492–1549) and Juan Boscán (1493?–1542).

17

Wyatt left no comments on his own poetry, even in the poetry itself, and we do not know exactly when, or with what aims in mind, his sonnets were written, though most of them seem to have been written before he left for Spain in 1537. He died prematurely of a fever, and did not live to see his poems published. He left a rich and varied collection of secular lyrics and religious verse, much of it occasional and some of it attachable to specific events at Henry VIII's court and elsewhere on his travels, and his sonnets form part of this, not apparently distinguished or set apart by Wyatt himself. Though we have a manuscript of his poems partly in his own hand, the Egerton MS, the order in which the sonnets appear there is not necessarily the order of composition.

From the thirty-three sonnets that can be attributed to Wyatt, it is clear that he took his inspiration from Petrarch and Petrarchist poets writing in Italian, and a number of his sonnets are translations. Others are adaptations or reworkings of ideas and phrasing, and others again seem wholly original. But right from the start, it seems, Wyatt chose not to copy the form of the Petrarchan sonnet, but instead invented a new one: instead of the two tercets, CDC DCD, of the Italian sonneteers, he chose to rhyme in a fresh quatrain and a couplet, CDDC EE. (One sonnet, 'The longe love, that in my thought doeth harbar', translated quite closely from Petrarch, *Rime*, 140, ends with CDC CDD, and one very old-fashioned and non-Petrarchan sonnet, 'Accusyd thoo I be', rhymes ABAB ABAB ABAB CC, and looks like an early experiment.)

Very few Italian or French sonneteers use the final couplet, but for British writers it had an immediate appeal, and has been used constantly ever since: a large part of the effect of a British sonnet depends on the couplet, and Wyatt's innovation thus needs some discussion here.

A rhyming couplet at the end of a sonnet (or of any short stanza) has a clinching effect, because the ear hears the second rhyme both as an echo and as a finish, rather like the chord progressions that are used in music to signal the end of a piece. There are couplets in a sense elsewhere in the sonnet – ABBA is a quatrain with a rhyming couplet in the middle – but the ear does not hear these as couplets because the sense of the sonnet is continuing past them. The last word of the sonnet, however, gains special finality if it rhymes with the end of the preceding line. The effect of clinching, of a decisive close, can be enhanced still further if the two lines at the end have more to do with each other in their sense than with the preceding lines – by sharing a figure of speech, for example, or being syntactically independent. This produces what is called a *sense couplet* to enhance the rhyming couplet.

Wyatt clearly liked the rhyming couplet, since all his sonnets end with one; but he did not always contrive a sense couplet to go with it. About half of his sonnets have sense couplets at the end: the sonnet quoted above (p. 16) is a good example of one that does not, but in his adaptation of Petrarch's *Rime* 190, Wyatt shows that he knew exactly how the final couplet could be used to strengthen the decisiveness of a sonnet:

> Una candida cerva sopra l'erba
>   verde m'apparve con duo corna d'oro,
>   fra due riviere all'ombra d'un alloro,
> levando 'l sole a la stagione acerba.
> Era sua vista sí dolce superba
>   ch' i' lasciai per seguirla ogni lavoro
>   come avaro ch 'n cercar tesoro
> con diletto l'affanno disacerba.
> 'Nessun mi tocchi,' al bel collo d'intorno
>   scritto avea di diamanti et di topazi:
>   'Libera farmi al mio Cesare parve.'
> Et era 'l sol gia volto al mezzo giorno,
>   gli occhi miei stanchi di mirar, non sazi,
>   quand'io caddi ne 'l acqua et ella sparve.

[A white hind on green grass appeared to me, with two golden horns, between two rivers in the shade of a laurel, at sunrise in spring. Her look was so sweet and proud that I left all my labours to follow her, like a miser whose delight sweetens the toil of his search for treasure.

'Let no one touch me,' was written in diamonds and topazes around her fair neck. 'It pleased my Caesar to set me free.' Now the sun had already passed midday, and my eyes were weary with gazing, but not sated, when I fell into the water, and she vanished.]

This mysterious and beautiful sonnet encodes Petrarch's first sight of his Laura, as he elsewhere recorded it, in Avignon at the confluence of the Rhone and the Sorgue, at matins on 6 April 1327, and his subsequent devotion to her image and memory. Wyatt's version of it is thought to encode his attempt to pay

19

court to Ann Boleyn, until warned off by his master, Henry VIII:

> Who so list to hounte I know where is an hynde;
>> But as for me, helas, I may no more:
>> The vayne travaill hath weried me so sore,
> I am of them that farthest cometh behinde.
> Yet may I by no means my weried mynde
>> Draw from the Diere: but as she fleeth afore,
> Faynting I folowe; I leve of therefore,
> Sithens in a nett I seke to hold the wynde.
> Who list her hount, I putt him owte of dowbte,
>> As well as I, may spend his tyme in vayne:
>> And graven with Diamondes in letters plain
> There is written her faier neck rounde abowte:
>> 'Noli me tangere for Cesars I ame,
>> And wylde for to hold though I seme tame.'

leve of: leave off; *Sithens*: since; *Noli me tangere*: 'Touch me not...': cf. John 20: 17

This quite different handling of the symbol of the untouchable deer (the deer is an international symbol, but the deer/dear pun works only in English) can be summarized by saying that, whereas in Petrarch's sonnet both speaker and hind vanish into empty space at the end, creating a final mystery, in Wyatt's sonnet the deer comes right up to speaker and reader at the end, and makes everything plain – she cannot be touched, because she already belongs to the King. Petrarch's deer is free, mistress of herself; Wyatt's deer is a slave who proclaims her status to all, and the final couplet (*am/tame* was a perfect rhyme in Wyatt's English) clinches the matter as the collar is clinched on her neck.

One might generalize this by saying that Wyatt's world in his sonnets is a secular world of practical courtly reality, a world of service, obligations, rights, petitions and answers, and struggle for personal security. When the rhyme couplet attracts a sense couplet, its effect is often to focus experience sharply, as here, in a clear and memorable, and often proverbial way. The sonnet in Wyatt's inventive hands acquires its British capacity to develop towards an epigram, proverb, or motto, and takes its place among the practical wisdoms of secular humanist court life.

5

Henry Howard, Earl of Surrey (1517?–1547)

Wyatt's spiky, tough, lively verse would be fine poetry even if he had not invented the British sonnet: his younger contemporary at the court of Henry VIII, Henry Howard, Earl of Surrey, might not have made it into histories of literature had he not been born to inherit an earldom. Surrey (as he is always known) has a smaller, technically competent but frankly duller body of work; but Richard Tottel, the publisher who printed Wyatt's poetry in 1557 after his death, puffed his volume by printing Surrey's poetry first in the book, and calling the whole volume *Songes and Sonettes, written by the right honorable Lorde Henry Haward late Earle of Surrey, and other*. Wyatt, as a mere knight, comes second, though with more than twice as much poetry. Tottel's anthology, universally known today as *Tottel's Miscellany*, was extremely popular in its century, as the first and for a while the only collection of contemporary British poetry, and the printing order did thus contrive to suggest to all its readers, including of course other, later poets, that Surrey and Wyatt in that order had somehow pioneered what Tottel called 'small parcelles...wel written in verse' – that is, short lyric and satiric poems.

If Surrey owes more to his rank than his Muse for this, he still made a notable contribution to the sonnet – it was he, not Wyatt, who found out the form that most later writers adopted if they did not want to use the Italian sonnet. He wrote about a dozen sonnets, some, like Wyatt's, translated or adapted from Petrarch, of which three have an odd rhyme scheme that he must have thought up for himself: ABAB ABAB ABAB CC. He cannot have liked this very much (with reason – six A and B rhymes tire the ear, and reduce the sonnet to a list), and his other sonnets all have his distinctive contribution: a change of rhyme at the second quatrain, keeping but building on Wyatt's idea of a change of rhyme at the sestet with his final couplet. For some reason he also chose alternating rhyme, as in the very early sonnets of Giacomo da Lentino and his fellows: ABAB instead of Wyatt's (and Petrarch's) ABBA. A Surrey sonnet thus runs: ABAB CDCD EFEF GG. This is much easier to write, since no rhyme sound is used more than twice, and there is interesting evidence that it had an immediate appeal: a considerable number of the 'and other' sonnets in Tottel's *Miscellany*, written by friends and acquaintances of Surrey, have his rhyme scheme rather than Wyatt's.

Now none of these writers knew how fashionable the sonnet was to become at the end of the sixteenth century in Britain: but the effect of this sonnet model of Surrey's invention was to give British writers much greater scope than their Italian and French counterparts. Henceforth they could choose Surrey's model (ABAB CDCD EFEF GG), or Petrarch's (ABBA ABBA CDE CDE), or Wyatt's as a halfway house (ABBA ABBA CDDC EE). Each of these has its own dynamic and its own way of structuring the thoughts and metaphors that go into it; and it is noticeable that experienced sonnet-writers, such as Sidney, Drayton, or Shakespeare, tend to settle upon one particular pattern. Despite translating and borrowing from French sonneteers, British poets made almost no use of the common French sonnet pattern, ABBA ABBA CC DEDE, and only one poet of any distinction, Edmund Spenser, invented another: ABAB BCBC CDCD EE.

Surrey paid tribute to Wyatt, whom he had known at court, as 'a hand that taught what might be said in rhyme;/That reft Chaucer the glory of his wit'. The comment is interesting because it shows Surrey aware that poets of his own day were following after – and implicitly competing with – previous poets. Something like a sense of literary development is evident here, and the competitive phraseology links literature to the other manifestations of princely prestige in the sixteenth century. But Surrey, who had made many enemies both through family politics and his own impetuous behaviour, was executed on a trumped-up charge of treason in 1547, and did not live to take the sonnet further. Richard Tottel did that for him: by foregrounding Surrey's sonnets (and Wyatt's) in his *Miscellany*, and by publishing in the same year (1557) Surrey's experiments with blank verse in his translations of Books 2 and 4 of Virgil's *Aeneid*, he made available a substantial body of verse to serve as models for later poets.

6

Anne Locke
(1530?–1595?)

An interesting example of Surrey's influence is the writer of the
very first sonnet sequence in English literature, Anne Locke,
who in 1560 published, appended to a volume of sermon
translations, 'A Meditation of a Penitent Sinner', a sequence of
twenty-six fluently written sonnets composed as a paraphrastic
meditation on Psalm 51, the 'Miserere'. All the sonnets are of
Surrey's type, and internal evidence in her text shows where she
encountered him: she was using Sir Thomas Wyatt's version of
Psalm 51 in his *Certayne Psalmes* of 1550, and Wyatt's book
happens to have a prefatory sonnet written by Surrey; this is it:

> The great Macedon that out of Perse chasyd
>   Darius, of whose huge power all Asie rong,
> In the rich ark dan Homer's rimes he placed,
>   Who fayned gestes of heathen princes song.
> What holy grave? what worthy sepulture
>   To Wiattes Psalmes should Christians then purchase?
> Where he doth paint the lively faith, and pure,
>   The stedfast hope, the swete returne to grace
> Of just David, by perfite penitence;
>   Where rulers may se in a myrrour clere
> The bitter frute of false concupiscence:
>   How Jewry bought Urias death full dere.
>   In princes hartes gods scourge imprinted depe
>   Ought them awake out of their sinfull slepe.

great Macedon: i.e. Alexander the Great; *dan*: Master; *song*: sung

This is an excellent sonnet: apart from the considerable
courage it must have taken to write this at the court of the
much-married Henry VIII, it has a ringing opening quatrain

reminding the reader that Alexander so venerated poetry that he carried Homer with him in a special box; but this is of course only the opening point in a developing argument: what then should the Christian do with the Psalms of David (now handily paraphrased by Wyatt)? The sestet then answers this by suggesting that these poems should be kept in the hearts of princes, so that they may learn to avoid lust, and finishes with Wyatt's own device of the final couplet used to enforce a maxim for princes – especially princes in a deep sleep.

The sonnet is remarkable for two witty pieces of enjambment, not at all common in early sonnets: as Alexander chases Darius out of Persia, the first line chases the sentence on into the next; and the 'swete return to grace / Of just David' occurs just at the junction of the eighth and ninth lines, the point that Italian writers called the *volta*, or 'turn'. The elliptical syntax of the second and third quatrains – 'Where he doth paint...' is a very loosely connected clause – gives a strong sense of the speaking voice of an orator urging a case, and the whole sonnet divides resoundingly into three sections: opening statement (ABAB), developed argument (CDCD EFEF), and conclusion (GG). There is nothing moving or plangent about this: just a vigorous sense of a speaking voice moving surely and fluently through a forceful argument.

Reading this, Anne Locke, who was a devout Calvinist married to a London merchant, absorbed the movement of thought that Surrey imparts: a balance between 'making a point' and developing one's ideas. It would be some time before British sonneteers reached near to Petrarch's fluency in this, but Locke's sonnet on Psalm 51 v: 12 ('Restore to me the comfort of thy saving helpe, and stablishe me with thy free spirit') would not disgrace any of the sonneteers of the reign of Elizabeth:

> But render me my wonted joyes againe,
>   Which sinne hath reft, and planted in their place
> Doubt of thy mercie, ground of all my paine.
>   The tast that thy love whylome did embrace
> My chearfull soule, the signes that dyd assure
>   My felyng ghost of favour in thy sight,
> Are fled from me, and wretched I endure
>   Senseless of grace, the absence of thy sprite.
> Restore my joyes, and make me fele again

> The swete retorne of grace that I have lost,
> That I may hope I pray not all in vayne.
> With thy free sprite confirme my feble ghost,
> To hold my faith from ruine and decay
> With fast affiance and assured stay.

tast that: sense that; *affiance*: attachment

Even at this early stage of our account of sonnet-writers, the reader may be acquiring a sense of what it is that makes a good or at least very competent sonnet; and using Locke's sonnet as an example, we can establish a few points for guidance. First, the movement of the thought should in some way relate to the structure established by the rhymes. Here Locke uses Surrey's ABAB CDCD EFEF GG rhyme scheme, and arranges for the idea in the first line to be repeated at the ninth, the *volta* of the sonnet: this draws attention to the fact that the octave is concerned with negative experiences in the past, and the sestet with positive ones to come. As the sonnet ends, the decay/stay rhyme is used to make the accomplishment of the sonnet coincide with the accomplishment of her faith. But second: within the octave and the sestet fluency can be gained by making the syntax work against the rhyme scheme: so Locke has made her sentences run in $3 + 5/3 + 3$ against $4 + 4/4 + 2$. Third, enjambment: if grammatical units – clauses, phrases, sentences – coincide with the line, an impression of regularity is given, though this can become monotonous. If units go on past the line end, and then stop halfway through the next line (enjambment with a medial caesura), there is a pronounced arrythmia: it is noticeable here that in the 'negative' octave Locke enjambs three times ('embrace/My cheerfull soule'; 'assure/My felyng ghost'; and the overarching 'the signes.../Are fled from me'), while in the 'positive' sestet every line coincides with a grammatical unit. The octave carries a sense of confusion, of words tumbling out in distress; the sestet is more settled and 'stayed'. Finally, the metre of the lines must normally respect the stresses of speech, since even in distress or confusion we do not misplace stresses on words. Wyatt very flagrantly does not respect speech stress, but his effects are so startling and so creative that it is usually supposed that he knew what he was doing. Surrey, by immediate contrast, is a smooth metrist, and Locke follows him. Only her fourth line stumbles, and the rather unnecessary 'did' suggests that she was having trouble with word arrangement.

Unfortunately for her reputation and influence, Locke published her sonnet sequence in 1560 at the end of a translation of one of Calvin's sermons, interesting and note-worthy in itself, but serving to mask the verse that followed, which accordingly does not seem to have been noticed by any of her contemporaries. It was thus Wyatt and Surrey alone who were given the credit as the first who 'having travailed into Italie ... greatly polished our rude and homely maner of vulgar Poesie from that it had bene before, and for that cause may justly be sayd the first reformers of our English meetre and stile'.[1]

Between 1560 and the return to England from Vienna in 1577 of a very intelligent young man with literary ambitions, Philip Sidney, a number of versifiers wrote and printed sonnets, which usually follow Surrey's model, and are mixed into miscellaneous lyric poems or inserted into prose narratives. Some writers, like Edmund Spenser in 1569, translated sonnets from French or Italian; but there is no sign in these decades that the sonnet is a special lyric form amongst lyric forms, and, indeed, the word 'sonnet' often seems to mean just 'short poem'. Then Sidney became interested in it, and very rapidly the sonnet acquired new genius and popularity.

7

Sir Philip Sidney
(1554–1586)

Sir Philip Sidney, knighted in 1582 and connected to the highest
families in the land, had barely begun his political career when
he died of a wound at Arnhem, without having seen any of his
own writing printed. But in the years when he was an impatient
young man waiting for great things, his energies went into
literature, and he produced three of the most interesting and
influential literary works of the late sixteenth century: a novel,
the *Arcadia*, a critical work, *The Defence of Poesy*, and a sonnet
sequence, *Astrophel and Stella*, all of which circulated in manu-
script among his friends and acquaintances.

The *Arcadia*, a complicated pastoral romance indebted to
Jacopo Sannazaro's work of the same name, is a prose narrative
with poetical interludes, in addition to which the characters
break into verse at moments of emotion. Like his contempor-
aries, he mixes sonnets with other verse forms in no clear
pattern, and only twice is a sonnet actually referred to as a
sonnet in the text. Yet there is evidence that he was interested in
the form, for, of the nineteen sonnets in the *Arcadia*, nine are of
Surrey's type, five are Italianate, and five have very strange
rhyme schemes that he must himself have invented, including
one rhymed entirely on '-ight' (AAAA AAAA AAAA AA). But in
among these 'passionate songs' are some sonnets that show
what Sidney was capable of even at this early stage:

> My true love hath my hart, and I have his,
>   By just exchange, one for the other giv'ne.
> I holde his deare, and myne he cannot misse:
>   There never was a better bargain driv'ne.

His hart in me, keepes me and him in one,
  My hart in him, his thoughtes and senses guides:
He loves my hart, for once it was his owne:
  I cherish his, because it in me bides.
His hart his wound receaved from my sight:
  My hart was wounded, with his wounded hart,
For as from me, on him his hurt did light,
  So still me thought in me his hurt did smart:
    Both equall hurt, in this change sought our blisse:
    My true love hath my hart and I have his.

cannot misse: cannot fail to keep

This witty, very singable, wholly delightful sonnet is supposed to be sung by a shepherdess in love: it is accordingly a little naive (one complete idea per line), utterly absorbed in love, as the ping-pong wordplay shows, and it uses the developmental structure of the sonnet to explain excitedly to anyone who will listen just what this heart exchange involves. But, like the posy of lovers' rings, it comes full circle, and, with a lovely rhyming precision that almost has the reader cheering, the last line completes the loop that joins the two hearts. The fact that Sidney was writing a novel in which the characters speaking the sonnet verses frequently found themselves in silly or extreme and absurd situations accustomed him to the exercise of wit and irony in verse, and in the *Arcadia* he even made an attempt at what he was later to do so much better in *Astrophel and Stella*: he created a minor character, Philisides, whose name shows him to be an alter ego, and who makes his infrequent appearances in the romance in a faintly absurd state of love-melancholy.

When he wrote his 'own' sonnet sequence, *Astrophel and Stella*, probably quite rapidly in the summer of 1582 (though the nature of a sonnet sequence is such that it can be assembled from sonnet components not originally intended to appear together), he was thus already a fairly sophisticated comic ironist with experience of dramatic narrative and dramatized passions in verse, and with an inclination to distance himself from himself, the narrating /I/ from the narrated /I/. As his character Astrophel (also spelt 'Astrophil') remarks in Sonnet 45, 'I am not I; pity the tale of me.'

The 'tale', which extends through 108 sonnets and eleven 'songs', shows the fruitless devotion of Astrophel to Stella, a married woman who seems inclined to love him but rebuffs his advances. There are narrative elements, but no continuous story. What occasioned this was an affection that Sidney apparently conceived for Penelope Devereux, daughter of the first Earl of Essex, whom he saw at court in 1581. She was betrothed to and then married Robert, Lord Rich, in November 1581. There is no evidence that any of the experiences or events related in the sequence ever happened; what does key Astrophel and Stella to Sidney's own life is Sonnet 24, 'Riche fooles there be', which by punning attacks Lord Rich in a wholly ill-mannered, even libellous, and as far as is known quite gratuitous way. Sidney allowed this sonnet to stand in the manuscript text he sent to his sister, the Countess of Pembroke (it was removed in the first, unauthorized printing of the sequence in 1591), but it would have no point at all even within his family unless Sidney had been known to have an attachment – whether reciprocated or not – to Penelope Devereux. So much it seems reasonable to assume.

All of the sonnets and all but one of the songs are written as if spoken by Astrophel himself (the eighth song has a narrator, but it is not implausible to imagine Astrophel for once narrating about himself in the third person). This obeys the convention established by Petrarch and followed by Wyatt, Surrey, Locke, and others, according to which what we read is what we should hear if we were present at the event the sonnet describes or represents – and this may include words spoken by others. Of course the speaker may choose to speak to us about something in his past, and many of Petrarch's sonnets are written in this more generally reflective voice. When the sonnets aggregate into a sequence, another possibility opens up: that the compiler of the sequence is the lover at a later, and possibly wiser stage, assembling an account of his own earlier sufferings or follies, for which, as Petrarch said, he may hope to find pity (from us? from his mistress?) if not pardon. Astrophel can thus be not just the lover hurtling from elation to dejection and back, but the poet trying to make sense of his own behaviour, and this overarching control of some kind of a narrative of passion holds the sequence together. In the second sonnet, Astrophel reviews his progress, both as lover and as the poet writing up his experiences:

Not at first sight, nor with a dribbed shot
  Love gave the wound which while I breathe will bleed;
  But known worth did in mine of time proceed
Till by degrees it had full conquest got.
I saw and lik'd, I lik'd but loved not,
  I lov'd, but straight did not at once what Love decreed:
  At length to Love's decrees I forced agreed,
Yet with repining at so partial lot.
  Now ev'n that footstep of lost liberty
Is gone, and now, like slave-born Muscovite,
  I call it praise to suffer tyranny,
And now employ the remnant of my wit
    To make myself believe that all is well,
    While with a feeling skill I paint my hell.

dribbed: off-target, accidental; *mine of time*: gradually; *partial*: unfair

Yet all this refracting of the self in the mirrors of narration would be nothing without Sidney's mastery of dramatic rhetoric. There is a marvellous bounce and verve in Astrophel's speech: as the sonnet above shows, the English is not exactly colloquial, but while tending towards the epigrammatic and compressed still manages to give the impression of excited speech. 'Ev'n that footstep of lost liberty/Is gone' is a sounding phrase that any politician might envy, but the preceding lines rattle along in the sort of iterative way in which we all manage climaxes when we are excited. Sidney's grasp of where to put the pauses of speech so as to avoid monotony on the one hand and incoherence on the other is little short of brilliant, and one feels that the great playwrights of the next decade, the 1590s, must have learnt a good deal about rhythm and syntax from him. As sonnet succeeds sonnet, Sidney keeps shifting Astrophel's moods and the objects of his attention, so that whether he is sad or happy, meditative or chatty, there is always a feeling of restlessness and impetus. The main rhetorical marker of this is apostrophe, the figure of speech that involves addressing oneself to a person or thing by name: 'Vertue, alas! now let me take some rest' (Sonnet 4). Constant exclamatory appeals to different personages make it appear that Astrophel cannot concentrate on anything (except Stella, of course) for more than fourteen lines at a time. The inevitable breaks between sonnets will tend to disperse the consciousness of the main speaker unless the writer makes determined attempts to achieve continuity – by repeating metaphors and symbols, by arranging sonnets in groups, and so forth. Sidney does not, because it is part of the ironizing of Astrophel's imagined devotion to Stella that Astrophel should appear disorganized by passion. The continuity of the sequence is assisted by the reiteration of Stella's name, and by the repetition of apostrophes, as noted already, but Sidney seems to have grasped in his own way the Petrarchan principle of the sonnet sequence as an organization of disorganized moments, rather as he created the *Arcadia* as a series of comic disorganizations of rather pompous or repressed characters. The sonnet clamps a kind of cage round extravagance, as when Astrophel, desperate for news of Stella, explodes on being unable to get the information he wants; the resulting sonnet (no. 92) contains the explosion very neatly:

> Be your words made, good Sir, of Indian ware
> > That you allow me them by so small rate?
> > Or do you cutted Spartans imitate?
> Or do you mean my tender ears to spare,
> That to my questions you so total are?
> > When I demand of Phoenix Stella's state,
> > You say, forsooth, you left her well of late.
> O God, think you that satisfies my care?
> > I would know whether she did sit or walk,
> > How cloth'd, how waited on, sigh'd she or smil'd,
> Whereof, with whom, how often did she talk,
> > With what pastime time's journey she beguil'd,
> > If her lips deign'd to sweeten my poor name.
> > Say all, and all well said, still say the same.

Indian ware: gold from South America; *cutted*: taciturn; *total*: brief, summary; *Phoenix*: unique, like the phoenix; *well*: thoroughly

This very dramatic sonnet, which constructs some feebly protesting social drone in its interstices, is one of many in *Astrophel and Stella* that dramatize some moment of failure or frustration or missed opportunity. Sidney's ability to construct a small scene, often involving, as here, another person whose replies can be inferred as the sonnet goes along, is a mainly comic talent that had not been seen much in British sonnet writing before him, but that became one of the resources of the sonnet (and of other lyric writing, such as Donne's) afterwards. There had been Italian sonneteers, as, for example, Cecco

Angiolieri (c.1260–1312?) and Il Burchiello (Domenico di Giovanni, 1404–1449), who were good at this, but Sidney is more likely to have picked up the technique from the French poet Pierre Ronsard (1524–85), and this kind of dramatic comedy is his own contribution to the British sonnet. Merely to address the beloved is not enough: to give the illusion that she (or any other addressee) is actually there requires a careful fragmenting of the sonnet to create spaces where the addressee might be imagined to reply, or try to – or perhaps, as here (Sonnet 47), simply walk past:

> What, have I thus betrayed my liberty?
>> Can those black beams such burning marks engrave
>> In my free side? or am I born a slave,
> Whose neck becomes such yoke of tyranny?
> Or want I sense to feel my misery?
>> Or sprite, disdain of such disdain to have?
>> Who for long faith, tho' daily help I crave,
> May get no alms but scorn of beggary.
>> Virtue, awake! Beauty but beauty is.
>> I may, I must, I can, I will, I do
> Leave following that which it is gain to miss.
>> Let her go! Soft, but here she comes! go to,
>>> Unkind, I love you not! O me, that eye
>>> Doth make my heart to give my tongue the lie!

beams: from Stella's eyes; *becomes*: suits; *sprite*: spiritedness; *Who*: i.e. I who; *Virtue*: integrity, self-respect; *Soft*: hold on!; *go to*: away!; *give*: accuse of (lying)

The idea of the sonnet as a place where things fall apart is possibly a logical development from the Petrarchan speaker, who is imagined as oscillating between extreme states of feeling; but it is also at odds with the humanist idea of persuasive rhetoric, where fluency, singleness of purpose (even in distress), and coherent argument dominate. Knowing that his readers will notice this, Sidney every now and then inserts a sonnet that discusses the problems of writing sonnets, as here, where the poet imagines part of his own mind appearing at his elbow, as it were, to question the whole enterprise:

> Come, let me write. 'And to what end?' To ease
>> A burthned heart. 'How can words ease, which are
>> The glasses of thy daily vexing care?'
> Oft cruell fights well pictured forth do please.

> 'Art not ashamed to publish thy disease?'
>> Nay, that may breed my fame, it is so rare.
> 'But will not wise men think thy words fond ware?'
> Then be they close, and so none shall displease.
>> 'What idler thing, then speake and not be heard?'
>> What harder thing then smart, and not to speake?
> Peace, foolish wit, with wit my wit is mard.
>> Thus write I while I doubt to write, and wreake
>> My harmes on ink's poor loss; perhaps some find
>> Stella's great powrs, that so confuse my mind.

fond ware: trash; *close*: secret/unpublished; *then*: than; *mard*: marred, spoilt

The trick so neatly executed in the last three lines, of writing an immaculately composed sonnet about the impossibility of writing sonnets while distressed by Love, is an old one – Petrarch's *Rime*, 74 is perhaps the inspiration for Sidney here – and as one looks closer it is clear that this 'unscripted' exchange between two bits of Sidney's mind (Sidney talking to Astrophel, perhaps) is actually rhetorically very highly organized, as in a stage play.

Indeed, when in 1591 the journalist and playwright Thomas Nashe wrote a preface for the first, and unauthorized, edition of *Astrophel and Stella*, he called it (by way of recommending it to the public) 'the tragicomedy of love ... performed by starlight' – a felicitous phrase, punning beautifully on Stella's name, and pointing to its appeal for Shakespeare's age. From Terence's *Andria* ('The Conscious Lovers') through to *Sleepless in Seattle* (The Unconscious Lovers, as one might say), the heartbreaks and the daftnesses of people in love have always been popular; but sixteenth-century court culture in Britain had not had its own love story until Sidney created the figure of Astrophel, witty, intelligent, but hopelessly adrift in love, the mirror for any fashionable young man, the Benedicks and the Darcys of the age. French sonneteers had been putting 'themselves' on display for some time, and the works of Ronsard, Desportes, du Bellay, Jodelle, and others of the Pléiade school in France were fairly well known in Britain in the last quarter of the sixteenth century.[1] Sidney happened to be the first British writer with sufficient talent to hit exactly the combination of wit, erudition, theatricality, and passion that his age liked, and he was widely regarded as the master of the love poetry of his age –

a mastership probably enhanced by his early death, appropriately lamented by fellow poets.

To someone who had read the relatively straightforward lamentations of Wyatt and Surrey and the plodding moralizing of the sonneteers of the 1580s, the appearance of so brilliantly conversational a piece as this must have been a fashion statement, locking into the exciting rhetoric of the new Elizabethan drama then beginning to be staged and just asking to be copied:

> No more, my deare, no more these counsels trie,
>   O give my passions leave to run their race:
>   Let Fortune lay on me her worst disgrace,
> Let folke orecharg'd with braine against me crie,
> Let clouds bedimme my face, breake in mine eye,
>   Let me no steps but of lost labour trace,
>   Let all the earth with scorne recount my case,
> But do not will me from me love to flie.
> I do not envie Aristotle's wit,
>   Nor do aspire to Caesar's bleeding fame,
> Nor ought do care, though some above me sit,
>   Nor hope, nor wishe another course to frame,
>   But that which once may win thy cruell hart:
>   Thou art my Wit, and thou my Vertue art.

once: once for all

This is a subtle and clever sonnet, written by someone very confident in his handling of its structure, and spoken by a character likewise by no means unsophisticated. It is first of all dramatic: that is, it suggests an immediate occasion, and without difficulty we can reconstruct what Stella has just said. She has told him that if he would only abandon his passion for her, he could find something worthy of his intellect and his nobility – 'Wit' means something like 'a very good head' and 'vertue' 'a worthwhile aim and reputation in life'. Astrophel then makes a passionate reply, marked by the repetition of 'Let...Let... Let...'. At the end of the octave, we may imagine Stella opening her mouth to reply, and being silenced as Astrophel rushes on with another passionate repetition (Nor...Nor...Nor...'), ending with a neat turn of her own words against her: '*Thou* art my Wit, and *thou* my Vertue art.' But it is not until we get this elegant chiasmus in the last line that we realize that these are the two words Stella has used, and that the whole sonnet follows on from them (though they are not of course there except by inference): Fortune's disgrace, the clouds, and the scorn of the earth all have to do with virtue (or the failure to pursue it); the insults of clever people and the futility of wasted labour have to do with stupidity, failure of wit. Then the sestet picks up Aristotle for cleverness (sitting above everyone) and Caesar for virtue (framing a famous, if tragic, course). And all this sounds as if it were a quick, spontaneous reply to Stella in the heat of a lovers' tiff.

Further, Sidney has allowed Astrophel to execute an elegant variation, in the octave of the sonnet, of an already well-known sonnet motif that itself comes from one of the most elegant and witty Latin poets, Horace, who, in an ode that most schoolboys in Sidney's day (and later) would know, declared, 'Place me on the steppes where no tree is refreshed by a summer breeze; on the side of the earth where clouds and bad weather break; place me in an uninhabited land scorched by the sun – I shall still love my sweetly smiling little chatterbox' (*Odes* I.24). Petrarch amplified this, adding 'Put me in obscurity or in great fame...' (*Rime*, 145) and Surrey translated Petrarch in his sonnet, 'Set me whereas the sun doth parch the green'. Sidney is echoing, not translating; but no educated reader could miss it, with the glow of self-approbation that recognizing a fashionable allusion brings.

8

Samuel Daniel (1562–1619)

There is a perfection of gesture and air in Sidney's sonnets that must have seemed the height of sophistication to a generation brought up on the rather heavy alliterative moralizing of Tottel's contemporaries. Sidney's family and friends knew what he was about in the late 1580s, but it was not until 1591 that a publisher printed his sonnets, in the unauthorized edition that had Thomas Nashe's preface, already quoted from. In the same volume, also printed without permission, were twenty-eight sonnets by a younger poet acquainted with Sidney's sister, Mary, Countess of Pembroke. This was Samuel Daniel, who was abroad in Italy at the time, and who, when he returned in 1592, angry at what he called 'the indiscretion of a greedy printer', promptly published the full version: *Delia. Contayning certayne Sonnets: with the complaint of Rosamond* (1592).

These 'certayne Sonnets' (*Delia* for short) formed a perfectly crafted fifty-sonnet sequence, and must have been written by the young Daniel after Sidney's death but under his influence and that of his sister. Daniel seems less vivacious than Sidney (we are talking here of the persona on display in the sonnets), but quietly erudite, versed in the literature of Italy and France – Daniel was well travelled and competent in French and Italian – and possessed of a kind of emotional steadiness, whose verbal enactment is in the long, singing line that he is the first to master in the British sonnet. This beautiful *cantabile* movement, shown here in Sonnet 32, is almost the contrary of Sidney's conversational brilliance, and it says much for Daniel's own talent that in Sidney's shadow he was able to do so well something so very different:

But love whilst that thou maist be loved again,
  Now whilst thy May hath fill'd thy lappe with flowers;
Now whilst thy beauty beares without a staine;
  Now use thy Summer smiles ere winter lowres.
And whilst thou spread'st unto the rysing sunne,
  The fairest flower that ever saw the light,
Now joye thy time before thy sweete be done,
  And Delia, thinke thy morning must have night,
And that thy brightnes sets at length to west,
  When thou wilt close up that which now thou showest:
And thinke the same becomes thy fading best,
  Which then shall hide it most, and cover lowest.
    Men doe not weigh the stalke for that it was,
    When once they finde her flowre, her glory passe.

The plangency of this sonnet, its capacity to bring tears to the eyes of quite hardened readers, is extraordinary: there is nothing here that has not been said a hundred times before, from Horace and Tibullus (the original Latin lover of Delia) to Swinburne, and yet Daniel makes an earnest and urgent and poignant melody out of a tissue of commonplaces. The structure of the sonnet flows with him almost unnoticeably: look at the very slight impulse of unexpectedness as one reaches the end of the octave, and stops, only to find the sentence running on; and on again, past the end of the ninth line to pull in the tenth. The imagery of the flower is of the simplest, but Daniel is confident enough in its strength to let the reader alone with the barest of paradoxes in lines 11 and 12, with their very Shakespearean wordplay (is 'fading' a noun or an adjective?). Then with his deft final couplet he brings together the world of the court, where women are goods on display, and the perfumers' harvest, where withered blossoms are discarded. There is a crisp irony under Daniel's lovesick manner.

Daniel seems to have been pleased with his sequence, for, though he reprinted it in four later editions (1594, 1595, 1598, and 1601), he made very few changes: there are fifty-seven sonnets in the 1601 edition, but the order is substantially the same, and the numerous textual alterations are mostly in the direction of greater metrical smoothness. Of all his contemporaries, he seems to have had, even as a young man at the beginning of the decade, the strongest sense of the coherence of a sequence: all his editions begin with a prologue sonnet and end with an epilogue one; and he used the Italian device of the *catena* ('chain') to connect a subgroup of sonnets (1592: 31–5) by making the last line of one the first line of the next. In addition, he used phrases to carry over from one sonnet to the next so that the reader was invited to make a twenty-eight-line poem out of two sonnets – a technique of pairing sonnets that Shakespeare seems to have noticed and imitated. If one wanted a textbook example of how to craft a sonnet sequence in Elizabethan England, Daniel provides it. His emotional range is limited – a steadfastly lamenting persona (ironic now and then) speaks the whole sequence – but his melodious fluency, imitated by other poets in the 1590s is the perfection of one kind of passionate rhetoric in the sonnet.

9

Edmund Spenser (1552–1599)

If Daniel is the Mozart of the sonnet, and Shakespeare its Beethoven (before you ask, Sidney is Vivaldi), then its Bach is Edmund Spenser: a poet of massive and slightly old-fashioned contrapuntal complexity who yet manages small forms with astonishing tenderness. In the midst of writing *The Faerie Queene* (1590–6), he became betrothed to Elizabeth Boyle of Kilcoran in Ireland, and wrote in her honour a sequence of eighty-eight sonnets (one is printed twice) and a long wedding poem, the *Epithalamion*. Published in 1595, the *Amoretti*, as they are called, were probably written between 1591 and 1594, when Spenser and his fiancée married.

After Wyatt and Surrey had gone to the trouble of inventing an English sonnet form that was easier to write than the Italian and French (ABAB CDCD EFEF GG), Spenser unobtrusively invented his own, much more complicated than anyone else's: ABAB BCBC CDCD EE – no one tried it after him, though it was actually used in Scotland before him, apparently independently, by poets writing in the court of James VI. The repetition of the rhymes increases the sense of flow in the sonnet, and in particular links the octave very strongly to the sestet (at the CC quasi-couplet) just at the point where the direction of the sonnet ought to change. In the hands of an inexperienced writer, this scheme could produce monotony: and indeed as Spenser's *Amoretti*, 34 gets under way, with one melodious point per line, one might wonder if this is a rather naive person talking. But as we reach the second quatrain and realize that we still have no main clause, the syntax suddenly, but without losing the singing quality, becomes much more difficult to follow (like the star, of course), and it will be quite a sophisticated reader who emerges into the sestet confident that she or he knows exactly what this apparently gentle, naive lover has just said:

> Lyke as a ship that through the Ocean wyde
>   by conduct of some star doth make her way,
> whenas a storme hath dimd her trusty guyde,
>   out of her course doth wander far astray,
>   so I, whose star that wont with her bright ray
> me to direct, with cloudes is overcast,
>   doe wander now in darknesse and dismay
> through hidden perils round about me plast.
> Yet hope I well that when this storme is past,
>   my *Helice*, the lodestar of my lyfe,
> will shine again, and looke on me at last
>   with lovely light, to cleare my cloudy grief.
>   Till then I wander, carefull, comfortlesse,
>   in secret sorow and sad pensivenesse.

plast: placed; *carefull*: i.e. full of cares

The delicately learned reference to Helice (spiral course, star in Ursa Major, jealous lover) enhances the sense of subtlety, and when one reaches the final couplet, normally the place for terseness, snap, and wit, the slight clumsiness of that last rhyme, imitating as it does the emotional stumbling of the lover, must be intentional.

Spenser knew Sidney, from whom he received some favours as a young man, and admired his work, including, of course, *Astrophel and Stella*, published just before he wrote his own sonnet sequence. (Spenser may well have read it in manuscript.) He shared Sidney's love of intricate narrative, but though capable of situational irony of enormous complexity, as *The Faerie Queene* shows, was naturally much more earnest and less inclined to be whimsical about himself than Sidney. As a consequence, his sonnet sequence has a speaker who takes himself and his love wholly seriously (as Petrarch did) but, lacking also Shakespeare's corrosive self-doubt, begins each sonnet as if its particular thought or experience were something new and fascinating. Even unpleasant experiences and setbacks are ushered through their sonnet with a kind of grave courtesy, and the intricate progress of the sonnet's structure (see above for Spenser's rhyme scheme) is the analogue of sweet reasonableness in love, something very rare in the sonnet's history. Greatly varied though the topics or subject matter of the *Amoretti* are, sonnets have a habit of settling down, the chained rhymes almost lulling in their quiet repetition. This – *Amoretti*, 65 – is in the fullest sense polite conversation between adults:

> The doubt which ye misdeeme, fayre love, is vaine,
>> that fondly feare to loose your liberty,
> when loosing one, two liberties ye gayne,
>> and make him bond that bondage earst die fly.
>> Sweet be the bands, the which true love doth tye,
> without constraynt or dread of any ill:
>> the gentle bird feels no captivity
> within her cage, but singes and feeds her fill.
> There pride dare not approch, nor discord spill
>> the league twixt them that loyal love hath bound:
> but simple truth and mutual good will
>> seekes with sweet peace to salve each others wound:
>>> there fayth doth fearlesse dwell in brasen towre,
>>> and spotless pleasure builds her sacred bowre.

loose: lose; *bond*: bound; *gentle*: well-born/well-natured; *spill*: destroy; *seekes*: seek; *pleasure*: sexual love

As a dignified and courteous response to a woman afraid of matrimony, this could hardly be bettered for honesty, good sense, and plainness, even if the allegory becomes a little heavy in the final couplet; and it is because her lover has the faith in her of which he speaks that the commonplaces of matrimony ring out as they do in the splendid sestet. Unlike Donne, whom we shall come to later, Spenser never fights against the structure of the sonnet, but flows with it, and the sureness with which everything falls into place is the analogue of his confidence, even through setbacks, in himself and his love.

In most of his writing, Spenser chose to adopt the voice of a simple, humble, or artless narrator, as here in the *Amoretti*, and his chained rhyme scheme is especially beguiling: the subtleties are all under a very smooth and melodious surface – consider, for example, the delicate syntactical ambiguity of 'the which true love doth tye'. Unlike Sidney, he has little liking for irony, and is always more formal than conversational, unlike Drayton: but those who love *The Faerie Queene* find the *Amoretti* subtle, inimitable, and, in their more gentle way, masterly. Any single sonnet may appear naive, but as one reads through the sequence – it is by no means certain that the order of the sonnets is Spenser's own – there is an accumulating richness of feeling and variety of viewpoint that makes Daniel, for example, seem oversimple. The rhymes themselves, and Spenser's command of alliteration, give a denseness to his melody, like a rich accompaniment to a simple tune, that no other sonneteer of his age exhibits. The following sonnet, apparently very simple in content and songlike in movement, seems to generate a kind of confusion and blockage through its alliteration and word patterning that is the mimesis of the speaker's growing bafflement, and the reader must decide for herself whether the final couplet makes the thickets of love clearer or even more impenetrable:

> Lackyng my love I go from place to place,
>> lyke a young fawne that late hath lost the hynde;
> and seek each where, where last I sawe her face,
>> whose ymage yet I carry fresh in mynd.
> I seek the fields with her late footing synd,
> I seeke her bowre with her late presence deckt,
>> yet nor in field nor bowre I her can fynd,
> yet field and bowre are full of her aspect.
> But when myne eyes I thereunto direct,
>> they idly back return to me agayne,
> and when I hope to see theyre true object,
>> I find my selfe but fed with fancies vayne.
>> Cease then myne eyes to seek her selfe to see,
>> and let my thoughts behold her selfe in mee.

(Amoretti, 78)

synd: signed

Any reader of *The Faerie Queene* will know the tremendous sophistication that Spenser can bring to the problems of seeing and seeking, of image, fancy, sign, and trace; but even the inexperienced sonnet reader should realize that among the echoes of that final couplet there is, as one might say, more than meets the eye.

The *Amoretti* are punctuated by sonnets referring to dates in Spenser's own life (as are Petrarch's *Rime)*, but they do not form any kind of connected narrative. The sonnets are followed by two very mannered Anacreontic poems about Cupid, and then by the glorious marriage ode, the 'Epithalamion': curiously, as critics have remarked, Shakespeare similarly ends his *Sonnets* with two (very bad) Anacreontic poems about Cupid, and then a very cynical long poem, 'A Lover's Complaint', which one might pedantically call a dysthalamion. It may be that these are two instances of a generic code that we have not learned how to read – sonnet sequences followed by lyric poems and a final ode are just too infrequent in British Renaissance literature for us to be sure what this sequencing meant. However, there is little doubt that the Epithalamion is the final poem of the *Amoretti*, in the sense that it is the climax to which they lead, rather as the last canzone, 'Vergine bella', is the climax of Petrarch's *Rime*. Though Spenser begins the *Amoretti* with an overview sonnet, asking the poems to commend themselves to his beloved, he does not restrict the 'leaves, lines and rymes' to the sonnets themselves, and, as he was married to Elizabeth Boyle by the time the volume appeared, it may well be that she, and we, are meant to read the sonnets as only part of an emotional exchange that culminates in the marriage itself. If so, Spenser, uniquely, has answered the fundamental problem of the Petrarchan sonnet, as it typically exists both in Britain and elsewhere: that its space is the space of disjunction, since the speaker is always responding to what Sidney wittily called an 'absent presence' – to paraphrase the child's rhyme, he meets a woman who isn't there, again and again, and, though the sonnet sequence can end formally with a valedictory sonnet, the separation of speaker and his desired Other is continued.

Spenser, it seems, recognized this, for he ends his sonnets with one of the most intensely realized absences in the whole of English literature, knowing, as we think, that he was about to relieve its negativity with the golden light of 'Epithalamion'. Like the dove of Psalm 55, distressed by evil tongues, Spenser's culver will come safely to rest; but to make sense of *Amoretti*, 86–9, we need to know that 'sacred peace may in assurance rayne' (*Epithalamion*, 354).

> Like as the culver on the bared bough
>   sits mourning for the absence of her mate:
> and in her songs sends many a wishfull vow
>   for his returne that seems to linger late,
>   so I alone now left disconsolate,

44

mourne to myself the absence of my love:
　and wandring here and there all desolate,
seek with my playnts to match that mournful dove:
Ne joy of ought that under heaven doth hove
　can comfort me, but her own joyous sight:
whose sweet aspect both God and man can move
　in her unspotted pleasaunce to delight.
　　Dark is my day, whyles her fayre light I mis,
　　And dead my life that wants such lively blis.

hove: occur; *wants*: lacks

This beautifully articulated sonnet matches phrases and sentences to lines and quatrains, but flows smoothly from start to finish with regular enjambments and a word order so entirely natural that one almost does not notice how complicated the rhymes actually are – more prominent is the repeated sound of 'late...late...late' in the octave, and then the sound of 'light' in the sestet, which of course enhances the meaning. Spenser's rhetorical power, acquired from *The Faerie Queene*, is so enormous that one wonders if he even noticed many of his own casual subtleties, like the pun on 'lively' in the last line. Certainly he showed many later writers, including Milton, how to run continuous speech through elaborate stanza forms without losing the sense of their structure. The reader who goes back to Sidney or Wyatt after reading Spenser will see at once that the earlier poets both found this difficult, but Spenser's training in explaining complicated ideas in narrative verse enabled him to present very varied ideas in varied tones of voice in the *Amoretti* without ever losing fluency.

As Spenser's own allegorical work shows, the quest for sight of the beloved, and acceptance by her, can be taken as an allegory or metonym of the quest for self-fulfilment in the world. The goals of being able to look upon someone, and be looked on reciprocally with favour, were as familiar to those seeking employment and reward in courtly society as they are in today's managerial structures, and the language of petition for access, sight, and regard (so delightfully played with in *Twelfth Night*, for example) in so many sonnets and sonnet sequences is at once relevant to private love, public office and court ceremonial. These 'loyal cantons of contemned love' have echoes far beyond the 'dead of night' outside Olivia's window.

10

Michael Drayton
(1563–1631)

Another very diligent petitioner was Michael Drayton, a longer lived contemporary of Shakespeare. Though a successful poet and dramatist, and one esteemed highly enough to be buried in Westminster Abbey, he never achieved the patronage, wealth, and courtly recognition that he thought he deserved; a portrait of him at the age of 50, used in his collected *Poems* of 1619, shows a laurel crown over a face definitely soured by experience. In his bids for employment and patronage he tried almost every literary genre with every likely patron, and came to sonnet writing early, publishing his sequence, *Ideas Mirrour*, in 1594. Much of this was prentice work, but he (and his contemporaries) thought well enough of the sequence to secure its reprinting, with revisions and additions, in 1599, 1602, 1605 and 1619.

His sonneteering technique developed throughout his life until the final printing of 1619, but Drayton remains one of the quirkiest of sonnet-writers. Some of his early sonnets are truly awful, unmetrical and incompetent to rival the worst writing of the 1580s; others (maybe only a few pages away) are witty, plangent, and moving, and might have been written by one of his great contemporaries. *Ideas Mirrour*, subtitled *Amours in Quatorzains*, is the work of a young poet with very little notion of what a sonnet or a sonnet sequence was: several of the poems are not quatorzains (fourteen-line stanzas) at all, and many of them are written in a bumpy and unpredictable mixture of 12-, 11- and 10-syllable lines. Though the sequence begins with a dedicatory sonnet and ends with a valedictory one, it has no further unity, and indeed reads like a kind of anthology of Elizabethan sonnet writing, as Drayton, desperate to be fashionable and original, imitates every rhetorical mannerism and conceit he can find in his contemporaries' work – principally from Sidney, Constable and Daniel, but also from Spenser.

As the sequence proceeded through later editions on into his collected *Poems* of 1619, Drayton wrote extra sonnets, removed old ones, reformed clumsy ones, and shuffled the order around with appropriate emendations. His very first, prefatory sonnet in *Ideas Mirrour* ('Read heere, sweet Mayd, the story of my wo...') becomes almost a valedictory sonnet in 1619: 'Yet reade at last the storie of my Woe...' Certainly Drayton retained the notion of the collection as a 'story', but over so long a period of time, what emerges finally in 1619 is a kind of retrospective of the English sonnet vogue, containing sonnets in all kinds of voices and attitudes. Drayton knew this, and liked to think of himself – that is, the speaker of the sonnets – as a mercurial personality: as he said in his prefatory sonnet in 1619,

> My verse is the true image of my Mind,
>> Ever in motion, still desiring change;
> And as thus to varietie inclin'd,
>> So in all Humors sportively I range:
>> My muse is rightly of the English straine,
>> That cannot long one fashion intertaine.

Petrarch himself, in his own prefatory sonnet (see above, p. 13) had spoken of 'the different styles in which I weep and argue', and attempted thus to control the internal variations between sonnet and sonnet by the notion of a disjointed or oscillating personality: single in its devotion to a mistress, but various in its responses to the frustration of that devotion. So Drayton: but for him, one suspects, there is liberation and self-proclamation in the sheer variety of gestures he can make, more so than for any other of his contemporaries, including Shakespeare.

Though he evidently regarded with disfavour some of his earliest and simplest sonnets (only twenty sonnets out of fifty-one in 1594 'got through' to the 1619 volume), he can still retain both the kind of seemingly naive rapture one associates with Spenser and the tough fantastic cynicism one finds in Donne and Shakespeare:

Bright starre of beauty, on whose eye-lids sit
 A thousand Nimph-like and inamor'd Graces,
The Goddesses of Memory and Wit,
 Which there in order take their severall places,
In whose deare Bosome, sweet delicious Love
 Lays down his Quiver, which he once did beare:
Since he that blessed paradise did prove,
 And leaves his Mothers lap to sport him there,
Let others strive to entertaine with Words,
 My Soule is of a braver Mettle made,
I hold that vile which Vulgar wit affords;
 In Me's that Faith which Time cannot invade.
  Let what I praise, be still made good by you:
  Be you most worthy, whilst I am most true.

(1619: 4; 1602: 66)

beare: 1602 beare; *did prove*: first tried; *vile*: cheap

Since to obtaine thee, nothing will me sted
 I have a Med'cine that shall cure my Love,
The powder of her heart dry'd, when she is dead,
 That Gold nor Honour ne'r had pow'r to move;
Mix'd with her Teares that ne'r her true-Love crost,
 Nor at Fifteene ne'r long'd to be a Bride,
Boyl'd with her Sighes, in giving up the Ghost,
 That for her late deceased Husband dy'd;
Into the same then let a Woman breathe
 That being chid, did never word replie,
With one thrice-marry'd's Prayr's, that did bequeath
 A legacie to stale Virginitie.
  If this Receit have not the pow'r to winne me
  Litle Ile say, but thinke the Devill's in me.

(1619: 15)

sted: help; *That*: i.e. 'her whom gold...'; *With*: along with; *winne me*: make me win

A whole history of Elizabethan and Jacobean verse, from pastoral artifice to urban cynicism, lies between these two sonnets, and both are part of Drayton's personality.

The word 'personality' is anachronistic when applied to the poetry of this age, for, though readers and critics assigned characteristics to authors – 'witty', 'delightsome', 'sweet', 'golden-mouth'd' (said of Drayton himself), 'crabbed', 'harsh' – these terms almost always described the style first, and the mind second, in accordance with the Renaissance humanist asump-tion that literature is a branch of rhetoric, and is outwardly directed to persuade others, not inwardly directed to express the self (however that entity may be understood). The sonnet, and by extension the sonnet sequence, however, was after Petrarch a place where in the guise of an attempt to persuade a beloved the passions of the self could be exhibited, and something like a self-reckoning (Drayton's 'summe of all my cares' in 1619. 3) offered to the public. Private prayers and meditations had long been a vehicle for this in a religious frame; the sonnet sequence offered an opportunity for self-display in a secular mode, but one that still fitted the concept of the self as constituted by client–patron relations: the speaker asks for reward (pity, love, recognition) and offers his immortalizing services as a poet:

> Where I to thee Eternitie shall give,
>   When nothing else remayneth of these dayes,
> And Queenes hereafter shall be glad to live
>   Upon the almes of thy superfluous praise...

(1619: 6)

Drayton is perhaps the sonneteer with the strongest sense of 'himself' as a collection of different moods and attitudes, and interesting simply because of that – or, as we might say using Drayton's own metaphor, on that account.

11

William Shakespeare (1564–1616)

Drayton and Daniel were both popular sonneteers in their own time, as their repeated revisions and new editions show; Shakespeare, despite his high reputation as a dramatist, attracted no attention as a sonneteer. When he published his sonnets – or allowed them to be published – in 1609, the sonnet vogue was all but over, and the 'mellifluous and honey-tongued Shakespeare' of the 1590s had moved into a kind of homoerotic dependency and a corrosive misogyny that must have been as difficult for his contemporaries ('wretched infidel stuff', one of them called it) as it still is for us, who have the advantage of certainty about his genius.

We know almost nothing, despite more than two centuries of research, about Shakespeare's composition of these 154 sonnets, or about their publication. From his plays and the literature of his day, we ought to be able to distinguish early sonnets from late ones; but no single sonnet has been convincingly dated, and they are stylistically very resistant to slotting into the various stages of his dramatic development: our best guess is that he reworked his sonnets continuously, so that early stylistic features are overlaid and interlaced with later ones. We know that by 1598 he had written enough sonnets to have a reputation as a sweet poet, because a contemporary, Francis Meres, tells us so; two of his sonnets were anthologized, most probably without his permission, in a collection, *The Passionate Pilgrim*, of 1599; and, as British poets did not write sonnets in enormous numbers, it seems likely that many sonnets that Shakespeare wrote in the 1590s carried over into his 1609 volume. But we cannot guess which these were, and, though many attempts have been made to rearrange the 1609 *Sonnets* into an order that would make some kind of sense – symbolic, biographical, dramatic – most editors accept the 1609 ordering as either what Shakespeare wanted or what he was quite content to allow.

Crucially, there are no sonnets at the beginning or the end that refer to the collection of 154 sonnets as a sequence or a narrative (cf. Drayton), and, though there are demonstrably a number of subsets of sonnets, linked by theme, by syntax, by figures of speech, we cannot even be certain that Shakespeare thought of the 1609 volume as a sequence in the usual sense: he may have thought of the collection as a miscellany, publishing it (as Katherine Duncan-Jones has persuasively argued in her introduction to the Arden *Shakespeare's Sonnets*[1] at a time when his income from plays was diminished.

Even the famous division of the 'sequence' (I shall now call it that) into two parts, Sonnets 1–126 addressed to the 'lovely boy', variously identified by critics, and Sonnets 127–54 addressed to the 'dark lady', is problematic, since many of the sonnets have no gender-markers, and might have been written originally to a person of either sex. The sequence does, however, open with seventeen sonnets clearly linked by topic and addressed to a boy or man, urging him to marry and father a child before it is too late; the second part opens with a sonnet addressing his 'mistress', and describing her as 'black' (dark haired and/or dark complexioned), a motif that then runs on through sonnets not otherwise gender-marked. Finally and probably most impor-tantly, there are four 'triangle' sonnets (42, 133, 134, and 144) in which the young man becomes sexually involved with the woman; and, though it is not provable that the 'she' of Sonnet 42 is the same person as the 'thou' of Sonnet 133, Occam's razor has a certain critical edge here. The boy or man is the speaker's social superior, accorded the kind of deference that the Petrarchan mistress usually exacts, and the mistress herself is either the speaker's equal or inferior, and is addressed with a mixture of adoration, cynicism and resentment not found in any other sequence in English.

We have therefore what looks like a suppressed narrative: sonnet sequences are not designed to tell stories, but, as Petrarch and Sidney and Spenser and others show us, they can be seen, and be intended to be seen, as moments in a story, and Shakespeare must have known this. An appreciable number of the sonnets, in both sections, address the beloved directly and also refer back to shared experiences of the speaker and his beloved (for example, Sonnet 40). They do not, however, identify any places, times, or persons, and have exactly the protocols of letters between people who already know what they are talking about. There are almost no external incidents (even the short horse ride in 50/1 is unusual) and no occasional poems – as in Petrarch's *Rime* – directed to other people. There is one sonnet that might be called religious (146) and several generally reflective or meditative sonnets addressed to no one in particular; and the whole sequence ends with two rather trivial love sonnets that have nothing at all to do with the preceding sonnets and do not even seem to come from the same world as the other 152. And the 1609 volume printed, after the sonnets, a long poem of 329 lines, apparently unfinished, spoken by a woman betrayed and abandoned by her lover, 'A Lover's Complaint'. The relationship between this and the preceding 154 sonnets is not clear.

Ever since the 1609 *Sonnets* were first subjected to disciplined scholarly and critical attention, by Edmond Malone in 1780, they have collectively proved extraordinarily resistant to analysis, whether biographical, historical or textual. No one doubts that individual sonnets are among the greatest ever written in English, displaying Shakespeare's mature control of some of the most difficult language attempted in our poetry; but how these sonnets should be read collectively remains quite undecided. The erotic themes are so unPetrarchan, and the ferocious intimacy of the speaker towards both a man and a woman so unusual, that, although clearly Shakespeare could have invented his material, most critics feel it to be from Shakespeare's own life. If so, the facts that the dedicatee of the volume is identified only by the initials 'W.H.' (usually thought to be William Herbert, Earl of Pembroke), and that many sonnets seem highly circumstantial without ever having yielded any dates, places, or persons to critical investigation, suggest that Shakespeare may have reworked earlier private poems late in his life, and removed all identifying material to avoid compromising his addressees.

In the first decades of the seventeenth century poetic

language was changing (as a review of Michael Drayton's sonnet publications shows) as older, simpler, and more idealizing forms of verse and expression were replaced by tougher, colloquial, and more cynical forms and styles. Pastoral imagery, much used by Petrarchan writers, developed a mannerist style, involving ingenuities of imagery that can seem precious or even decadent. All these elements are present in Shakespeare's sonnets, and often a sonnet will start in a simple mode and modulate into something tougher and less innocent, as in Sonnet 35 (reproduced here, as the other sonnets quoted, from the 1609 text – any other text must have editorial assumptions built in):

> No more bee greev'd at that which thou hast done,
>   Roses have thornes, and silver fountaines mud,
> Cloudes and eclipses staine both Moone and Sunne,
>   And loathsome canker lives in sweetest bud.
> All men make faults, and even I in this,
>   Authorizing thy trespas with compare,
> Myself corrupting salving thy amisse,
>   Excusing their sins more than their sins are:*
> For to thy sensuall fault I bring in sence,
>   Thy adverse party is thy Advocate,
> And 'gainst my selfe a lawfull plea commence,
>   Such civill war is in my love and hate
>   That I an accessary needs must be,
>   To that sweet thief which sourly robs from me.

compare: comparison; *civill*: also means 'polite'

[*Editors are agreed that there is something wrong with this line, and have suggested amending one or other 'their' to 'thy' or 'these'.]

Shakespeare's sonnets are so various and surprising that it is risky to select one as a sample: this sonnet does, however, exhibit many of his characteristics. First, he uses a traditional sonnet form, ABAB CDCD EFEF GG, which he never varied, except when he repeated a rhyme (for example, Sonnet 135). As in early British sonnets, he prefers to keep his quatrains distinct, with a punctuation point at the end of each. He is very fond of the clinching final couplet, but in this sonnet, unusually, the material of the couplet starts in the line before. He even prefers to make each line a point or idea, and enjambs very seldom – it appears that line 5, above, ends with a subject ('even I') that will have a later verb; but it does not. He seems to have had no interest in altering the structure of the sonnet as it was in the early 1590s. Second, his extraordinary force comes mainly from lexical and phonological intensifications: for example, 'compare' and 'amiss' have been ruthlessly converted into nouns, and phonological repetition in lines 9–10 plays havoc with meaning: since 'sensual' and 'sense' are linked by repetition of a syllable, their meanings are challenged: does 'in sense' by any chance also mean 'incense', that is, perfume to banish the odour of corruption? And since 'adverse' and 'advocate' start with the same syllable, is the law corrupt – how comes it that what is against one ('adverse') resembles that which is for one ('advocate')? One's uneasy sense that an advocate can be either for or against as he is paid is then picked up by the paradoxes of lines 11–14, by which the speaker is shown to be divided against himself.

This, indeed, is the third characteristic of the *Sonnets*: though they are often addressed to the beloved (male or female), they are by the end about the speaker himself, and specifically about the sense of self that he has. This is frequently anguished and uncertain (Shakespeare seems happiest in his speaker's role when he is simply promising to immortalize his patron) in a way that might fairly be called existential or, at the end of the twentieth century, deconstructive. Ambiguation of language, through reconstruction and deconstruction of its components, phonological, lexical and syntactical, in an almost Joycean manner is constant, and lines such as

> For as you were when first your eye I eyed

> (104. 2)

are not blunders, but part of a strategy of tortured self-explication. In a conventional Petrarchan sequence, the lady is a paragon of beauty and virtue, and disdains her imperfect lover:

> Oft have I told her that my soul did love her,
> And that with tears; yet all this will not move her.

> (Samuel Daniel, 1591)

In Shakespeare's sequence, both the man and the 'dark lady' are flawed, and their imperfections and betrayals become a kind of mirror of his own inadequacies. The lover who responds to perfection by expressing devotion in perfect rhetorical form responds to imperfection by a disjointed expression of inadequacy.

The conventional Petrarchan sonnet (and, of course, Petrarchan poetry in other forms) had always dealt in absolutes: absolute devotion, perfect beauty, complete disdain, eternal love. Even Sidney, with his strong sense of the quirkiness and absurdity of human behaviour, still respects Petrarchan idealism: Stella is 'the only planet of my light,/Light of my life, and life of my desire'. But Shakespeare's highly complicated rhetoric often seems to work to undermine those traditional idealisms: the word 'seems' (which so annoyed Hamlet) is prompted by the reflection that if, as suggested above, Shakespeare's *Sonnets* are an accumulation over more than a decade, then many early sonnets may have been written in a spirit of Petrarchan idealism, which as we now read them become corroded or subverted by the cynicism of later work. A good example to show how the reader is uncomfortably manœuvred by his or her own reading experience is Sonnet 53, a famous and much anthologized sonnet:

> What is your substance, whereof are you made,
>> That millions of strange shaddowes on you tend,
> Since every one hath every one one shade,
>> And you, but one, can every shadow lend:*
> Describe *Adonis*, and the counterfeit
>> Is poorly imitated after you;
> On *Hellens* cheeke all art of beautie set,
>> And you in *Grecian* tires are painted new:
> Speak of the spring and foyzon of the yeare,
>> The one doth shaddow of your beautie show,
> The other as your bountie doth appeare,
>> And you in every blessed shape we know.
>> In all externall grace you have some part,
>> But you like none, none you, for constant heart.

every one: Q: one, Q: *Adonis* and; conterfet; *tires*: robes; *foyzon*: harvest Q: none you for

(*This is one of the best examples of Shakespeare's quite uncanny ability to say apparently quite simply, and apparently quite comprehensibly, something that turns out to be very hard to explain. The young man is so wonderful that everyone tries to imitate him: since one's shadow is (Platonically) an imitation of oneself, the young man can be said to lend everyone their shadow. No other Renaissance sonneteer habitually does this.)

This is a version of the Petrarchan conceit, going back to Plato (*Rime*, 248), that the beloved is a sort of pattern book, created by

God or Nature, from which those who want to find out what any excellence is can take examples; and if we came across it ascribed to Samuel Daniel, or Michael Drayton, we should think it clever but straightforward. Even knowing it to be by Shakespeare, we might read it in company with Sonnets 52, 54, and 55 without noticing more than that the beloved's beauty seems to be bisexual – Adonis and Helen in one.

But if we read 'through' the *Sonnets*, and come to this after, say, Sonnet 20 and Sonnets 33–43, and know that Sonnets 57 and 58 are coming, then we are sensitive to the implications of imagery and of wordplay, and to the resonance of words such as 'shadows' and 'counterfeit'. Suddenly, one realizes that the last couplet may contain one of these grammatical transformations of which Shakespeare, uniquely among sonneteers, is so fond: 'like' may be both a preposition and a verb, and the last line, which appears to mean 'For constancy, you are without parallel', may also mean 'You have so various a nature that you have no fondness for any constancy, and no one esteems you for constancy in return.' This in turn seems to satisfy the rhetorical expectation of the previous line: the follow-up to 'In all external grace you have some part' should be 'but in internal graces you have no share'. And then, of course, the whole vocabulary of shadows, shapes, painting, showing, and appearance, and the slightly sinister sexual ambiguity of the comparisons – Adonis was disastrously self-absorbed, and Helen adulterous ('What *is* your substance?') – links up with the deadlier sonnets, such as 87–99, and the melodies of Daniel or Drayton fade away.

Even if we assume that Shakespeare permitted the *Sonnets* of 1609 to appear as they did, we cannot safely assume that he would have approved of such a reading, or have thought that his poems would be read cumulatively and with cross-references. Some kinds of sequentiality he must have either arranged or tacitly approved: Sonnets 1–17, already referred to, form a subsequence on the topic of fathering a child to keep alive the qualities of the beloved – a theme so singular in sonnet writing that sonnets on it would not occur casually in a writer's work, and a theme also that does not appear again. Then there are a number of sonnet pairs, where the second sonnet answers or continues from its predecessor, and there are larger groups, such as 91–96, where the verbal and also topical links between sonnet and sonnet are so close as to suggest that they were written as a unit. Whether Shakespeare arrived at these subgroupings by reworking originally disparate sonnets, or whether he had sets of sonnets previously composed for incorporation into the collection, we simply do not know. But most of the sonnets in the collection work very well as independent poems, while also lying next to or among other sonnets that could affect their meanings.

This indeed is a problem – or perhaps a flexibility – unique to sonnets. Each sonnet must stand on its own, but is capable of being joined to its fellows in various ways. If we know that the sonneteer intended the collection to be read as one, then we can be more confident in connecting sonnets together, as when we read *Astrophel and Stella*; or we can avoid doing so, as when we read Sir Thomas Wyatt's sonnets. No other literary form has this tension between independence and connectedness of its parts – unless, perhaps, a collection of letters might be felt to behave in the same way.

Does it matter that Shakespeare has left us no instructions, implied or expressed, for reading his *Sonnets*? Certainly there are a number of sonnets so self-contained, and with imagery so well established, that they are not much affected by what surrounds them – for example, Sonnet 60 ('Like as the waves make towards the pebbled shore') or Sonnet 147 ('My love is as a fever'). But if, on the other hand, Shakespeare himself placed Sonnet 74 ('But be contented when that fell arest') next to Sonnet 73 (the much anthologized 'That time of year thou maist in me behold'), he must have known that the second sonnet unravels the first, and that he was in effect writing one twenty-eight-line poem. In the text below, the spelling and punctuation are given exactly, save for one misprint, as in the Quarto of 1609, to avoid importing editorial decisions other than those of Shakespeare's own printer; but I have closed the gap, to invite the reader to read 'them' as one poem.

> That time of yeeare thou maist in me behold,
>   When yellow leaves, or none, or few doe hange
> Upon those boughes which shake against the could,
>   Bare ruin'd quiers, where late the sweet birds sang.
> In me thou seest the twi-light of such day,
>   As after Sun-set fadeth in the West,

Which by and by blacke night doth take away,
  Deaths second selfe that seals up all in rest.
In me thou seest the glowing of such fire,
  That on the ashes of his youth doth lye,
As the death bed, whereon it must expire,
  Consum'd with that which it was nurrisht by.
    This thou percev'st, which makes thy love more strong,
    To love that well, which thou must leave ere long.
But be contented when that fell arest,
  Without all bayle shall carry me away,
My life hath in this line some interest,
  Which for memoriall still with thee shall stay.
When thou revewest this, thou dost revew,
  The very part was consecrate to thee,
The earth can have but earth, which is his due,
  My spirit is thine the better part of me,
So then thou hast but lost the dregs of life,
  The pray of wormes, my body being dead,
The coward conquest of a wretches knife,
  Too base of thee to be remembred,
    The worth of that, is that which it containes,
    And that is this, and this with thee remaines.

[*ruin'd* Q: rn'wd]; *Without all bayle*: with no chance of bail; *that*: i.e. this line

If the first fourteen lines are a single poem, then they are a sad, or even pathetic, attempt by a greying Shakespeare to exhort his lover to love him more intensely since time is short. But if it is read immediately with what follows, then the emphasis alters: the young man's view of Shakespeare, expressed in these sounding elegiac metaphors, is seen as a mistake, and he is rebuked for lavishing his love upon the mortal part; what matters is the spirit, which the verse that he is now reading preserves for ever. The second sonnet is actually a *correction* of '[what] thou perceivest' in the first sonnet, and the meaning of the very first line alters: not a sad 'It is, alas, quite likely that I look elderly to you' but a confident assertion that 'Certainly, I may look old to you, but if all you see in me is just the wreckage of time, then remember that..'.

Shakespeare, indeed, seems to have written more paired sonnets than any of his contemporaries – there are twelve pairs in the collection, if we include the two above, 73 and 74, and one of these, 91 and 92, is probably a triplet, including 93. In no case is the link between the sonnets formal, that is, involving the repetition of rhymes or of line (repetition of a single rhyme word, of course, does not pair sonnets), but there is always a thematic and usually also a verbal link, though rarely one so strong as to disable the second sonnet from standing alone. The twelve pairs are 5 and 6, 15 and 16, 27 and 28, 44 and 45, 46 and 47, 50 and 51, 67 and 68, 73 and 74, 89 and 90, 91 and 92, probably with 93, 113 and 114, and 135 and 136. Beyond these there are numerous small groups of sonnets that might be read as one continuous poem (e.g. 33, 34, 35) or just as so many sonnets that happen to be on the same subject. Yet this linking is so much more pronounced in Shakespeare than in any other writer of his age as to make one think that, despite his failure to provide any prefatory or valedictory sonnets, he actually understood the nature of the sonnet sequence rather better than many writers who did take an overview of their own collection.

Just as in Shakespeare's plays (particularly in the earlier plays) there are 'great speeches' that make a point, strike an attitude, or argue a case, but also form part of an ongoing dramatic whole, so in the *Sonnets* there are single sonnets which work on their own, but also lead on to other sonnets that develop from them. Exactly how many there are, and how they connect up, is something that critics continue to argue, but Shakespeare clearly did group sonnets in this developmental way, or at least allowed his publisher to assemble them so. He must therefore have thought of the sonnet experience as an assemblage, not just of moments (like speeches), but of developments of moments, rather like the scenes of a play, which can be discontinuous one with another, but all reflect aspects of a developing dramatic reality.

But, rather strangely for the leading dramatist of his age, he allows no voice but 'his own' to speak in the *Sonnets*. He could write dialogue sonnets – there is an excellent one in *Romeo and Juliet*, I. v – but no other voice intrudes on his soliloquies in the 1609 collection. He does not even, as Sidney is wont to do, start a sonnet as a reply to something just said (but not of course actually there). Even the various questioning sonnets, which challenge the beloved in some way, do not unavoidably posit him or her as present to hear them said. There is something very lonely about Shakespeare's sonnets; and, if all Petrarchan sonnets are, by the very nature of Petrarchan love, concerned with absence, Shakespeare's seem more obsessed than most of his contemporaries with what Donne, quintessencing Jacobean melancholia, called 'absence, darkness, death, things which are not'. Shakespeare's speaker is constantly faced with the quandary that the absence of the beloved – whether physically removed or emotionally distant – is a negation of himself, trammelling the self in various kinds of notness – counterfeiting, staining, wavering, thieving, ignorance, and silence. Sonnet 92, following directly from 91, is a tissue of all these, and ends, of course, in silence with the word that sums them all up: 'not':

> But doe thy worst to steale thy selfe away,
>   For tearme of life thou art assured mine,
> And life no longer then thy love will stay,
>   For it depends upon that love of thine.
> Then need I not to feare the worst of wrongs,
>   When in the least of them my life hath end,
> I see, a better state to me belongs
>   Then that which on thy humor doth depend.
> Thou canst not vex me with inconstant minde,
>   Since that my life on thy revolt doth lie.
> O what a happy title do I finde,
>   Happy to have thy love, happy to die!
>   But whats so blessed faire that feares no blot?
>   Thou maist be false, and yet I know it not.

then: than

The echo of Othello in the last line merely adds to the sombre desperation of this writhingly unhappy, but still very clever, piece of sonnet argument. Its apparently naive organization, two lines to each point, with no enjambment and no suspended sentences, intensifies the sense of someone stumbling, like Othello, through a series of exhausted rationalizations of something gone dreadfully wrong.

Though many of the sonnets are innocent of any such darkness, and in that resemble the sonnets of Shakespeare's contemporaries, the whole sequence (but remember that there is no proof that Shakespeare intended us to read it as a whole sequence) is coloured by the tone and rhetoric of the sonnets of self-criticism and self-deconstruction:

> That God forbid, that made me first your slave,
>   I should in thought controule your times of pleasure,

60

Or at your hand th'account of houres to crave,
  Being your vassail bound to staie your leisure.
Oh let me suffer (being at your beck)
  Th'imprison'd absence of your libertie,
And patience tame, to sufferance* bide each check,
  Without accusing you of injury.
Be where you list, your charter is so strong,
  That you your selfe may priviledge your time
To what you will, to you it doth belong
  Your selfe to pardon of selfe-doing crime.
    I am to waite, though waiting so be hell,
    Not blame your pleasure be it ill or well. (58)

to crave: should crave

[*By putting in or taking out commas after 'tame' and 'sufferance' editors make their own sense of this very baffling line. The 1609 version is also quite sensible: 'and having tamed my patience, endure each frustration up to the limit of toleration'.]

There must be hundreds of sonnets in which the lover declares himself the slave of the beloved; but very few like this. Every vestige of Petrarchan romantic imagery has been bleached away, and what is left is an arid, even bloodless protest against indulgence, caprice, cruelty, arrogance, and malice, to which the only proper response is silence. The abstract language is so thin and bitter that it is hard to realize that there are any metaphors here at all: but line 6 shows, by its very intense difficulty, how ruthlessly fast these metaphors of slavery and cruelty are being driven through the sonnet. There is a kind of masochistic ambivalence in all these terms: the reader will certainly, in the final couplet, hear the first four words as spoken aloud – but in what tone of voice? The speaker even throws away, as if it were of little moment, the information that the beloved's pleasures may be indifferently either corrupt or innocent – 'be it ill or well' – as if the beloved's moral behaviour were of no concern.

That the poet who could write 'Shall I compare thee to a summer's day?' (Sonnet 18) could also write this, apparently to the same person, suggests either that the *Sonnets* of 1609 are a miscellany of poems written over a considerable period of time, during which relationships changed, or that they were reworked and left in juxtapositions that emphasized the nearness of love and hate as a means of enforcing the ambivalence of loving. We do not know; but we do know that the kind of savage, and often very self-absorbed, uncertainty about self that riddles (in both senses) the language of so many of the sonnets is also in the great plays of the early seventeenth century: *Hamlet, Timon, All's Well,* and above all *King Lear.* Sonnet 58 could well have been spoken by Lear to Goneril in bitter mockery.

Writing sonnets was clearly important to Shakespeare: his is the longest single collection of sonnets among his contemporaries, and indeed one of the longest in British literature; and his sonnets do not seem to have been used elsewhere, in the sense that we do not find quatrains or sections of his sonnets in the mouths of characters in his plays; nor did he, as many of his contemporaries used to, translate, paraphrase, or adapt from other sonneteers, whether British or French or Italian (see below on Drummond of Hawthornden). His sonnets seem very much his own, and if it is easy to pull out sonnets here and there that are in the manner of Sidney, or Daniel, or Constable, or Drayton, still what Rosalie Colie called 'Shakespeare's particularly brainy, calculated incisiveness'[2] is like no one else's, and appears to mirror the themes, preoccupations, images, and rhetoric of some of the great plays of the period 1600–10.

Because the *Sonnets* appear to offer a glimpse into Shakespeare's mind, they have always attracted critical attention as the voice of the man behind the fiction of the dramas, and the literature on the *Sonnets* is enormous. In the later nineteenth century, and particularly in anthologies, those sonnets that showed calmness, an elegiac sense, and a meditative approach to life were preferred ('Thou smilest, and art still,' said Matthew Arnold in one of his own sonnets); the twentieth century, especially in its postmodern phase, has contrarily asserted Shakespeare's problematization of himself, his homoerotic themes, his violence of language and his questioning of the nature and function of rhetoric. The reader is referred, in the Bibliography, in the first instance to editions of the *Sonnets* that themselves give good critical guidance and ample bibliographies for further study.

So far in this account, the sonnets discussed have been entirely secular, on the theme of Petrarchan love or in some sort of reaction to it. Most British sonnet sequences were indeed

Petrarchan, but huge numbers of single sonnets were written on occasional subjects, dedications, commemorations, satires, philosophical or meditative, many even simply domestic, like Sir Robert Ayton's adaptation of a French sonnet 'Upon Tobacco':

> Forsaken of all comforts but these two,
>   My fagot and my pipe, I sit and muse
>   On all my crosses, and almost accuse
> The heavens for dealing with me as they do.
> Then hope steps in, and with a smiling brow
>   Such cheerful expectations doth infuse
>   As makes me think, ere long I cannot choose
> But be a grandee, whatsoe'er I'm now.
>   But having spent my pipe, I then perceive
>   That hopes and dreams are cousins: both deceive;
> Then make I this conclusion in my mind:
>   It's all one thing, both tend unto one scope,
> To live upon Tobacco and on hope –
>   The one's but smoke, the other is but wind.

fagot: burning wood; *cousin*: pun on cozen = deceive

This is an elegant French trifle, translated for good measure in the French sonnet form, rarely used independently by British writers (ABBA ABBA CC DEED) (Ayton was a Scot, for whom 'brow' and 'now' would rhyme with 'two' and 'do'.) The impromptu, conversational tone of this is of course a learnt skill, like any other rhetorical pose, but this persona is well adapted to muse on more serious matters than tobacco: several poets of the time wrote religious sonnets in which the speaker converses with his God, and the elaborate display of one's feelings towards a mistress, like a peacock's tail feathers, is replaced by a humbler and more sober self-accounting before God. Henry Constable wrote several 'Spiritual Sonnettes' about 1594 (not printed until 1815); Henry Lok, the son of Anne Locke, mentioned above, was a prolific, and not very good, religious sonneteer (he published *Ecclesiastes* in 1597); William Alabaster, about 1597, wrote a long sequence of religious sonnets, again not printed until much later, in 1959; but the most celebrated religious sonneteer is John Donne.

12

John Donne
(1572–1631)

As is well known, Donne's secular poetry, entitled 'Songs and Sonets' in the edition published after his death, contains no sonnets; his sonnets appear in his 'Divine Poems'. (The textual situation is complicated, and the reader is referred to the Bibliography for further study.) There are two sets of sonnets: the first set is what is known as a 'corona sequence', written about 1609, and the second is a collection of nineteen sonnets, usually known as the 'Holy Sonnets', which were circulated in different numbers and states in Donne's lifetime, and which are not demonstrably a sonnet sequence.

'La Corona' (so titled in the 1632 edition of Donne's *Poems*) is a sequence of seven sonnets, each sonnet beginning with the line that ends the previous one, as Samuel Daniel had done in *Delia* (1592). The first sonnet's opening line is the last line of the last sonnet, producing the circular effect that gives this type of sequence its name. Corona-sequences, which can be very elaborate indeed, were popular in sixteenth-century France and Italy, but are almost non-existent in Britain, for no obvious reason – unless it was that, like the sestina, another popular European form hardly used in Britain, they are just very difficult to write. (The reader may like to look at a modern example: George Macbeth's 'A Christmas Ring' (*The Burning Cone*, 1970), which is a corona sequence including the device known in Italy as the *sonello magistrale*, or 'master sonnet' – a final sonnet (added to a fourteen-sonnet sequence) made up of the first lines of all the preceding sonnets. Even Donne, with only seven sonnets, declined to try this.)

Sonneteers quite often make the difficulty of writing sonnets an analogue of the difficulty of remaining faithful to a disdainful lover (see, for example, Shakespeare's Sonnets 85, 115); Donne very neatly makes the successful completion of his crown ('corona') of praise into the proof that God has raised him out of his low spirited condition – the proof that God's mercy has worked is that Donne can say that it has in an intricate 'text' – 'text' etymologically means 'a woven thing'. Sonnet 1 begins:

> *Deigne at my hands this crown of prayer and praise*
> Weav'd in my low devout melancholie,

and the seventh sonnet ends:

> Oh, with thy owne blood quench thy owne just wrath,
> And if thy holy Spirit, my Muse did raise,
> *Deigne at my hands this crowne of prayer and praise.*

Each sonnet is complete in itself – indeed, each sonnet carries its own title – but, because of the reiteration of lines, is also chained to its fellows in the circle of praise. The iterations have an almost liturgical force, but that of course is much to the point in a religious sequence.

Nevertheless, Donne did not attempt corona linkage again, and his remaining nineteen 'Holy Sonnets', while containing some of the finest religious sonnets in English, are not obviously a sequence. They were written probably between 1610 and 1619, and did not all appear together, either in print or in manuscript, until collected by modern editors. Technically, they are remarkably adventurous, as Shakespeare's sonnets are not: using a mixed Italian and English form, ABBA ABBA CDDC/CDCD EE, Donne employs violent disturbances of rhythm, syntax, and word order to create a persona beating his way through thickets of doubt. Constant enjambment, hyperbaton (abnormal syntactical order), and eclipsis (omission of words) flourish in lines that have only the most tenuous connection with normal iambic pentameters. Shakespeare's metaphorical ruthlessness and density Donne does not have: he is a sonnet revolutionary of schemes rather than of tropes, and this difference should be clear if the reader will set Shakespeare's Sonnet 58 (printed above) alongside Donne's eleventh sonnet (in the 1632 *Poems*):

Wilt thou love God, as he thee! then digest
  My Soule, this wholsome meditation,
  How God the Spirit, by Angels waited on
In heaven, doth make his Temple in thy brest.
The Father having begot a Sonne most blest,
  And still begetting, (for he ne'r begonne)
  Hath deign'd to chuse thee by adoption,
Coheire to his glory,'and Sabbaths endless rest;
And as a robb'd man, which by search doth finde
  His stolne stuffe sold, must lose or buy'it againe:
  The Sonne of glory came downe, and was slaine,
Us whom he'had made, and Satan stolne, to unbinde.
  'Twas much, that man was made like God before,
  But, that God should be made like man, much more.

The reader may like to try an experiment with the above sonnet and Shakespeare's Sonnet 58: if both are read aloud, the average non-expert listener will quickly detect that Shakespeare's sonnet is in verse, but will probably have very little idea what it means; Donne's sonnet, though tough, is quite intelligible, but it is possible to hear it through without realizing at all that it is in verse – until, perhaps, the final couplet strikes the ear. Donne writes (allowing for the seventeenth-century idiom) in very plain English, the metaphors of which are relatively few and usually biblical; his difficulty and toughness come almost entirely from dislocations of rhythm and word order. The sonnet from the third line to the twelfth is one long sentence controlled by the construction 'digest / This meditation: how ... God the father ... [how] The father begetting ... and [how] The Sonne of glory ...'. Once the missing words are inserted and the syntax reordered, the difficulties vanish; no amount of such rearranging will help the metaphorical denseness of Shakespeare's sonnet. Similarly in the final couplet the sense of difficulty is almost wholly metrical: Donne has run the stresses of the last line considerably counter to the metrical stresses, so that the normal iambic pattern suggests

But THAT God SHOULD be MADE like MAN, much MORE,

whereas one's sense of the sense of this very simple English line gives

BUT that GOD should be MADE like MAN, MUCH MORE.

The clash of these two rhythms, the first intuited and the second required, produces just the sense of stumbling that the paradox of God's action effects in the mind. There is no such dislocation of rhythm in Shakespeare's sonnet, where the deceptively natural coincidence of speech and verse rhythms masks even more the problems of the metaphors.

Donne was, by the time he wrote his 'Holy Sonnets', a professional preacher, and by all accounts a most effective one: whether his sonnets are addressed to himself, in a meditative fashion ('Why are we by all creatures waited on?') or to another person, such as God, his soul, or others ('Spit in my face you Jewes, and pierce my side'), his sonnets have the control of pitch, rhythm, stress, and timing that would be second nature to a preacher addressing an audience. But, because they are also sonnets, they have a schedule to which the performer must adhere, and, as when a practised tightrope walker appears to stumble, there is often a feeling that the urgency of the speech has so dislocated things that the speaker will not manage to reach the far side – for example, what appears to be a regular opening line – 'Spit in my face you Jews, and pierce my side' (/ x x / x / x / x /) – actually has to be spoken with quite a different arrangement of stresses: 'SPIT in MY face, you JEWS, and pierce MY side'. Donne was notorious, in Ben Jonson's words, 'for not keeping of accent', but what appears to be wildness or indiscipline makes sense if treated as the controlled outburst of a preacher working his audience up.

Everywhere in Donne's 'Holy Sonnets' these techniques operate to give a strong sense of the urgency of the struggle to understand God's dealings with the human soul. Donne used these devices throughout his verse, both sacred and secular, and it has to be said that Shakespeare, if he avoided them in his *Sonnets*, employed them brilliantly in his later dramatic verse. In this, the two poets were catching the fashion of the decade (1600–10), in which there was a new interest in the fragmenta-tion of the mind under stress (Hamlet, Lear, Timon, Bosola, Burton's *Anatomy of Melancholy*, and so on) mirrored by rhetorically contrived fragmentation of dramatic and lyrical discourse in literature: both the insouciance and cynicism of light and witty verse, and the intensity of psychologically analytical serious verse, found this new way of representing the poetic persona congenial. The sonnet was by then becoming old-fashioned, and many writers just continued its strict form as it had been, even while making, like Drayton, alterations of manner. Donne actually altered the form, by destroying almost all its regularities other than those of rhyme scheme and length (fourteen lines). Two sonnet-writing contemporaries noticed this – one, George Herbert (1593–1633) imitated him in his own quieter way; the other, William Drummond (1585–1649), did not, but found his own kind of distinction. And finally, as we shall see, the writer who most profoundly influenced the British sonnet in the nineteenth century, John Milton, synthesized the sonnet techniques of Donne and Drummond. Had it not been for these three, the sonnet would probably have halted its career with the unsuccess of Shakespeare's 1609 collection.

13

George Herbert (1593–1633)

George Herbert, a family friend of John Donne, is much better known as a religious poet than as a sonnet-writer: he wrote no sonnet sequences, and most of the seventeen sonnets he did write appeared only in his posthumous poems, *The Temple* (1633). Herbert was extremely devout, and two of his earliest sonnets, written as a New Year's gift to his mother in 1610, show him casting a disapproving eye on contemporary secular poetry and, in so doing, demonstrating how he himself could use the sonnet form:

> My God, where is that ancient heat towards thee,
>   Wherewith whole showls of Martyrs once did burn,
> Besides their other flames? Doth Poetry
>   Wear Venus Livery? only serve her turn?
> Why are not sonnets made of thee? and layes
>   Upon thine Altar burnt? Cannot thy love
> Heighten a spirit to sound out thy praise
>   As well as any she? Cannot thy Dove
> Out-strip their Cupid easily in flight?
>   Or, since thy wayes are deep, and still the same
>   Will not a verse run smooth that beares thy name?
> Why doth that fire, which by thy power and might
>   Each breast doth feel, no braver fuel choose
>   Than that, which one day Wormes may chance refuse?
>
> Sure Lord, there is enough in thee to dry
>   Oceans of Ink; for, as the Deluge did
> Cover the Earth, so doth thy Majesty:
>   Each cloud distills thy praise, and doth forbid
> Poets to turn it to another use.

Roses and Lillies speak thee; and to make
A pair of Cheeks of them, is thy abuse.
  Why should I Womens eyes for Chrystal take?
Such poor invention burns in their low mind
  Whose fire is wild, and doth not upward go
  To praise, and on thee Lord, some Ink bestow.
Open the bones, and you shall nothing find
    In the best face but filth, when, Lord, in thee
    The beauty lies in the discovery.

showls: shoals; *still*: always; *chance*: happen to

Written at the end of the year in which Shakespeare's *Sonnets* were published – it is tempting to think that, since no new love sonnets had been printed since 1605, it was a reading of Shakespeare's sonnets that so irritated the young Herbert – these two sonnets are formally much more inventive than Shakespeare's: he would never have written a sonnet in which, as in Herbert's second, the first quatrain runs over into the fifth line, let alone have perpetrated the enjambments and medial pauses of the first sonnet. Clearly Herbert knows what he is doing, since he suddenly smooths his first sonnet out just at the point where he asks, 'Will not a verse run smooth that beares thy name?'

Young as he was, these two sonnets are astonishingly advanced, if we regard the incorporation of the irregularities of spontaneous speech into the tight sonnet form as progress. There is no contemporary sonneteer from whom he could have learnt this transgressive writing: his predecessors, though often willing to extend a sentence across the line end or even over the end of a quatrain, respected the major divisions. Sidney, who enjambs fairly freely in his sestets, keeps his octaves regular; Shakespeare, as we have seen, hardly ever passes over a conventional boundary in the $4 + 4 + 4 + 2$ structure, and even Drayton, quirky as he is, is not formally particularly adventurous. Herbert might have seen John Donne's corona sequence (written about 1607), but even that would hardly have taught him to break up the line/sentence congruence of the conventional sonnet as completely as he does above, particularly in the first sonnet of the pair. These sonnets look forward to Donne's 'Holy Sonnets' of the second decade of the century, and beyond that to Gerard Manley Hopkins in the nineteenth century.

Herbert influenced his contemporaries not at all by his sonnets, since they did not appear till after his death: their interest to us is that they show where one of the century's best lyric poets, discontented with the secular Petrarchan sonnet, could take the form. His sonnet 'The Answer', much less urgent and distracted than Donne's, shows several virtues not commonly practised together: the use of the syntax and phrasing of common speech, like Sidney; the maintenance of a very even iambic rhythm, like Shakespeare; the use of very extensive enjambment and medial pauses, like Donne, and the use of plain but profoundly compressed metaphors, avoiding both vulgarity and pedantry, again like Shakespeare. The effect is one of steadiness and weightiness combined with simplicity and intensity. An Italian would have recognized this combination of qualities, and called it *gravità*, much admired among the European poets of the sixteenth and seventeenth centuries, and not of course confined to sonnets:

> My comforts drop and melt away like snow:
>> I shake my head, and all my thoughts and ends
> Which my fierce youth did bandie, fall and flow
>> Like leaves about me; or like summer friends,
> Flyes of estates and sunne-shine. But to all,
>> Who think me eager, hot, and undertaking,
> But in my prosecutions slack and small,
>> As a young exhalation,* newly waking,
> Scorns his first bed of dirt, and means the sky
>> But cooling by the way, grows pursie and slow
> And setling to a cloud, doth live and die
>> In that dark state of tears: to all that so
>>> Show me, and set me, I have one reply,
>>> Which they that know the rest, know more than I.

ends: aims; *summer*: 'fair-weather'; *prosecutions*: achievements; *means the sky*: means to reach; *pursie*: bloated, sluggish; *show*: publicly repute; *set*: esteem

[**Exhalation*: a shooting star, then thought to be generated from the earth itself, 'breathing out' fiery matter.]

This quiet but masterly sonnet is organized round the rhetorical figure of aposiopesis, the sudden breaking-off of the sense because the speaker has, in the urgency of his feelings, lost the thread of what he was going to say. Here the speaker appears to lose control at line 12, where at the word 'tears' the sense falters, and he has to go back to the beginning, 'to all who...', and start again. To enforce this disorganized spontaneity the phrases and sentences begin and end out of phase with the quatrains of the sonnet: a $4 + 4 + 4 + 2$ rhyme scheme, ABAB CDCD EFEF EE (or just possibly EAEA EE), is set against syntactical units that run $4\frac{1}{2} + 2\frac{1}{2} + 4\frac{1}{2} + 2\frac{1}{2}$, so that, though the rhymes are very firm, clinched by the internal A-rhymes of 'show', 'know', and 'know' in the couplet, it is actually very hard to grasp the internal organization – how many readers, looking at the sonnet, assume before counting that the sestet begins with the words 'As a young exhalation'? Yet there is no doubt that the sonnet has momentum, climax, and resolution, and that the speaker is, unlike Sidney's Astrophel or Shakespeare's alter ego, firmly in control of his experience: passionate in his exposition but rational in his conclusion. Though the subject matter is penitential rather than erotic, there is something very Petrarchan about this, but it is the Petrarch of the sonnets after Laura's death that is recalled here.

Petrarch (to return to him as the master of the European sonnet for a moment) very rarely took the phrasing of a sonnet across its major boundaries, and what one might call the freeing-up of the sonnet, as shown in Herbert's examples, was something that occurred in the sixteenth and seventeenth centuries in France and Italy and Britain. Nevertheless he was aware of the effect of enjambment, and particularly of enjambing across the sonnet's major break, between lines 8 and 9. This is the point at which (no matter what the rhyme scheme) the sonnet formally conceptualizes the idea of break, antithesis, or change, and an emphasis can be secured, as here in Petrarch's *Rime*, 326.· (For the benefit of readers who cannot follow Italian easily, obliques are inserted to show where phrase and sentence endings occur.)

> Or ài fatto l'estremo di tua possa,\
>   o crudel Morte,\ or ài 'l regno d'amore
>   impoverito,\ or di bellezza il fiore
> e 'l lume ài spento\ et chiuso in poca fossa;\
> or ài spogliata nostra vita\ et scossa
>   d'ogni ornamento et del sovran suo onore;\
>   ma 'l fama et 'l valor, che mai non more,
> non è in tua forza;\ abbiti ignude l'ossa,

ché l'altro à 'l Cielo,\ et di sua chiaritate
  quasi d'un più bel sol s'allegra et gloria;\
  et fi' al mondo de' buon sempre in memoria.\
Vinca 'l cor vostro in sua tanta vittoria,
  angel novo, lassù di me pietate,\
  come vinse qui il mio vostra beltate.

[Now you have done your utmost, \o cruel Death;\ now you have impoverished the realm of Love,\ now you have put out the flower and light of beauty,\ and shut it up in a small grave;\ now you have ruined our life\ and taken from it every ornament, and chief glory;\ but fame and worth, which never die, are not within your power;\ take for yourself the bare bones, for Heaven has the rest,\ and is glad and proud of its clearness as of a brighter sun;\ and in the world of the good it will always be remembered.\ In its triumph, new angel, let your heart yield there above to pity for me,\ as your beauty conquered mine here.]

Rhetorically, this sonnet has quite a simple structure: the first part deals with the triumph of Death, and the second with the triumph of reputation and virtue, in the soul of Laura, who is the 'new angel' addressed in the plea for intercession that concludes the poem. Conventionally, the sonnet should list the various trimphs of Death ('Now you have…now…now…'), and then turn, at the ninth line, to the triumphs of Heaven ('But fame and worth…'). What Petrarch does, however, is to arrange his sentences so that the ninth line starts rather later, after the word 'ossa' (bones): one realizes then that what 'turns' in this sonnet is not the subject matter (Death/Heaven) but the speaker's attention. Up to the eighth line the speaker is talking to Death, and everything is negative, even fame and worth, in the negative sense that Death does not have them; after that, the speaker's attention turns to the 'new angel', and away from what is dark and bleak to what is bright. With a gesture of contempt, but without pausing in his speech, so great is his certainty, he dismisses Death with his bare bones, because ('ché') Heaven has everything else. As always, the sonnet is a dramatization of a moment, here a moment of rage against Death (shown by the enjambments) turning into a feeling of trust and hope.

Had Petrarch written sonnets of this transgressive kind more often, the history of the sonnet might have been different; as it was, most Petrarchan imitators, in Britain at least, still thought of the sonnets as a collection of points arranged 4: 4: || 4: 2, with a pronounced shift of some kind after the second quatrain.

Herbert and Donne are the first to try to break this frame. John Milton, who was probably the sonnet-writer most influential upon the poets of the nineteenth century, may well have read the sonnets of Herbert and Donne; he certainly knew the sonnets of Spenser, Sidney, and Shakespeare, though he did not imitate them. The poet from whom he does appear to have borrowed, if only slightly, was a much more conventional sonneteer: William Drummond of Hawthornden (1585–1649). Only two sonneteers published in quantity in the decade of Shakespeare's death: Drummond, with seventy-seven sonnets in his *Poems* of 1616, and a further twenty-six in his *Flowers of Zion* (1623); and the second British woman to publish a sonnet sequence, Lady Mary Wroth, whose *Pamphilia to Amphilanthus*, circulating in part some seven or eight years earlier, was published in 1621. We shall consider her before turning to Drummond (who admired her poetry).

14

Lady Mary Wroth (1587?–1651?)

Lady Mary Wroth, though a tough, resourceful, and formidable woman in many ways, was not a particularly inventive sonnet-writer. She derived her model of writing from her uncle, Sir Philip Sidney: like him she wrote a long prose romance, *The Countess of Montgomerie's Urania*, similar to Sidney's *Arcadia*, containing a number of poems uttered by the characters, of which several are sonnets; and like him she also wrote a sonnet sequence spoken by one of the characters in the prose romance, *Pamphilia*, who, like Philisides/Astrophel, seems to be a version of herself. As in *Astrophel and Stella*, the sonnets are interspersed with songs, and she adopted Sidney's favoured sonnet forms, using the Italian ABBA ABBA CCD EED (with variants) and the mixed Italian–English ABAB ABAB CDCD EE (with variants) about equally. In the final published version, her eighty-three sonnets and songs appear in four subsequences, arranged, with songs interspersed, as 48 + 1 + 10 + 14 + 9, and the name 'Pamphilia' as a signature, occurs at the end of the group of forty-eight and at the end of the set of nine. She is also one of the few British sonnet-writers to use the corona form: the group of fourteen sonnets is a full corona sequence, though the linkages are not well done.

Her attachment to the old-fashioned Petrarchan rhetoric (which her uncle had poked fun at thirty years before) is so strong that it is very difficult to locate any distinctive female voice: only two of the sonnets (41 and 42 in the first group) identify the beloved as male, and, for the rest, the Petrarchan rhetoric and imagery are, as the Italian women poets of the sixteenth century demonstrated, equally applicable to the passions and distresses of both sexes addressed to a beloved of either sex. There is no kind of narrative, and, if she can be said to have a distinctive manner, it is that her sonnets tend to have a good, if sometimes rather compressed, analytic centre, using the structure of the sonnet to tease out the nature of a distress. Her sonnet endings are then frequently inconsequential or not adequate to the material before them, as here, in a sonnet that owes something to *Astrophel and Stella*, 54 (the punctuation of the 1621 edition has been amended: it is heavy and often nonsensical):

> How well, poor heart, thou witness canst I love,
>> How oft my grief hath made thee shed for tears
>> Drops of thy dearest blood, and how oft fears
> Borne testimony of the pains I prove!
> What torments hast thou suffered, while above
>> Joy thou tortured wert with racks which longing bears,
>> Pinched with desires which yet but wishing reares,
> Firm in my faith in constancy to move:
> Yet is it said that, sure, love can not be
>> Where so small show of passion is descried,
>> When thy chief pain is that I must it hide
> From all, save only one who should it see.
>> For know, more passion in my heart doth move
>> Than in a million that make show of love.

(Sonnet 36)

prove: experience; *but*: mere

A sequence that shows Lady Mary at her best, but that might escape notice, is 'Lindamira's Complaint'. This is a set of seven sonnets occurring in the text of her prose romance, *Urania*, spoken by a minor character forsaken by her lover, whose fictional career in the text is, as the editor of Wroth's poems points out, very close to the author's own. There are still echoes of Philip Sidney, but the thought moves tersely forward, colloquially, often with an epigrammatic snap to it, and showing no sign of the technical problems that occur in *Pamphilia to Amphilanthus*:

> O Memory, could I but lose thee now,
>> At least learn to forget, as I did move
>> My best and only thoughts to wait on love,

76

And be as registers of my made vow.
Could I but let my mind to reason bow,
    Or see plain wrongs, neglects and slightings prove
    In that dear Sphere which as the Heavens above
I prized, and homage to it did allow.
  Canst thou not turn as well a Traitor too
  Since Heaven-like powers teach thee what to do?
Canst thou not quite forget thy pleasures past,
    Those blessed hours, the only time of bliss,
    When we feared nothing but we time might miss
Long enough to enjoy what's now off cast.

Sphere: i.e. her lover; *as well*: as good (as her lover)

This sonnet, with three others in the set, is a French sonnet (ABBA ABBA CC DEED), a form that Sidney, and hardly any one else, occasionally used, and it shows Lady Mary to have been observant of sonnet forms. Those that Sidney did not employ, such as the Spenserian and the Shakespearean, she did not use either, but her uncle's experiments gave her a wide choice. And, just as her uncle's sonnet sequence referred to events in his own life, though not explicitly, so Lady Mary's poems, and her novel, were thought among her contemporaries to be written 'à clef' – that is, using fanciful classical names for real people known to the author, though no authorial key has been found or is known to have existed.

15

William Drummond (1585–1649)

Like Lady Mary Wroth, William Drummond of Hawthornden wrote most of his sonnets fairly young, publishing them in 1616 in a three-part sequence of seventy-seven sonnets with twenty-four songs and madrigals interspersed. The first group of sonnets, fifty-five in number, address a living mistress, called Auristella; the second group of thirteen mourn her after her death; and the third group, titled *Urania*, of nine sonnets and four songs, are in praise of heavenly love. Drummond himself was proud of having written his sequence with a division into sonnets *in vita* and *in morte*, as Petrarch had done, and he correctly pointed out that no other Italian or British writer had done this. This attracted attention from his editors, and (particularly because Drummond married very late in life, in 1632, when he was 47), it has been persistently suggested that his sonnets were written to a young woman to whom he was betrothed, but who died on the eve of their marriage. She was named in the eighteenth century as a Miss Cunningham from a family in Fife, Scotland, with which Drummond had certainly corresponded. It is worth saying here that, attractive as this idea is, the discovery some forty years ago of an epitaph sonnet written by Drummond to the memory of 'the right Worthie and Vertuous Euphemia Kyninghame' actually makes the story unlikely: her death occurred on 23 July 1616, and that is much too late for the mourning sonnets to have been composed for her – they appeared in an early issue of the *Poems* about 1614.

The motive behind Drummond's poetry, sonnets included, seems to have been entirely literary, something unusual in the

British Renaissance, when sonnets were commonly written to gain patronage and favour, which even sonnet-writers of high rank could use in their fashion. Sir Philip Sidney, probably, and Lady Mary Wroth almost certainly, since she was herself a patron, did not write for patronage: and Drummond, though the eldest son only of a humble knight, had both a very adequate estate and a retiring temperament. The first enabled him to acquire a formidably good private library in several languages, and the second made him happy to remain on his estate near Edinburgh all his life, without national honours or political office.

The particular relevance of this to Drummond's sonnet writing lies in something we have not so far mentioned about Petrarch, whose long shadow fell on Drummond as on others: in the year 1337, ten years after he said he first set eyes on his Laura, Petrarch bought a small house and garden north of the city of Avignon, where he (and Laura) were living, at Vaucluse at the source of the River Sorgue, an extremely wild and remote spot, and the antithesis of the cosmopolitan city of Avignon. He lived there intermittently until about 1350, and, though he was no recluse, there is no doubt that he genuinely liked the place, and incorporated the landscape into his poetry. The myth of the man who is happy in rural solitude, free from the corruptions and cares of city life, is known to literary scholars and others as the *Beatus ille* ('Blessed is the man') myth or motif, and has been popular in literature since the time of the Roman poet Horace (65–8 BC), who had a small villa in the Sabine Hills, near Rome, and wrote about his life there in his poems (his 'Second Epode' supplies the title of the myth). Petrarch combined this with the solitude of the pining Petrarchan lover, and with a metaphorical and symbolic skill that even today has few rivals (one thinks of Rilke, another lover of solitude) turned the landscape of the Vaucluse countryside into the analogues of his own feelings and sites of his visions.

Drummond liked to think of himself in this half-Horatian, half-Petrarchan fashion, and one of his sonnets, 'Thrise happie hee, who by some shadie grove/Farre from the clamorous world doth live his owne...', is translated from the Italian poet Marino, who in his turn is paraphrasing Horace. He obligingly left a record of the books he read in the years when he was writing his own sonnets, and from that, and from comments scattered among his surviving correspondence and notes, it seems that he thought of himself as competing with his British and European contemporaries, such as Ronsard, Boscan, and Bembo, in a kind of distillation of Petrarch and Petrarchan motifs. Accordingly, his sonnets are, to a much higher degree than those of any of his British contemporaries, translations, quotations, paraphrases, and echoes from all that he was reading in English, French, Italian, and Spanish at the time. Critical ideas of originality or personal statement will simply not work in Drummond's verse, even though many of his poems contain only the briefest of allusions.

As an example, we may take the following sonnet, the twenty-fifth in the 1616 volume, here in its 1614 version:

> Dear quirister, who from these shadowes sends,
>   Ere that the blushing Dawne dare showe her Light,
> Such sad lamenting Straines, that Night attends
>   (Become all Eare), Starres stay, to heare thy plight:
> If one whose griefe even reach of thought transcends,
>   Who ne'er, not in a Dreame, did taste delight,
> May thee importune who like case pretends,
>   And seems to joy in woe in Woe's despite –
> Tell me (so may thou Fortune milder trie,
>   And long, long sing) for what thou thus complains,
> Since Winter's gone, and Sun in dappled Skie
>   Enamoured smiles on woods and flowrie Plaines?
>   The bird, as if my questions did her move,
>   With trembling wings sobbed forth, 'I love, I love.'

quirister: chorister, i.e. the nightingale; *attends*: waits; *stay*: stop; *not*: other than; *pretends*: shows

The reader who, at this point, thinks he or she has read something like this before and reaches for a dictionary of quotations (try Milton, *Comus*, 557–67) will be responding with exactly the sort of intertextual awareness that Drummond invites, and indeed must have cultivated. Sonnet writing, as I have said, is a cumulative experience, but Drummond deliberately purchased and read poetry so that he could accumulate the voices of others in his verse. Milton, who also wrote a nightingale sonnet, of course came afterwards; but before this sonnet there are at least two voices just in the first four lines: Petrarch himself, and Pierre Ronsard (in his *Œuvres* of 1560):

Quel rosignuol che sì soave piagne
  forse suoi figli o sua cara consorte,
di dolcezza empie il cielo et le campagne,
  con tante note sì pietose e scorte...

(Rime, 311)

piagne: piange;

[That nightingale who laments so sweetly, maybe for his children or for his beloved consort, fills the sky and the landscape with sweetness in many pitiful, well-tuned notes...]

Rossignol mon mignon, qui dans cette saulaye
  Vas seul de branche en branche à ton gré voletant,
  Et chantes a l'envy de moi, qui vais chantant
Celle qu'il faut toujours que dans la bouche j'aie...

[Dear nightingale, who flutter through these willows alone, from branch to branch at your own sweet will, making me envious with your song as I go singing of her whose name must be always on my lips...]

Then there is a strong echo – literally of the sound of the words as well as of the ideas – of lines from Sidney's ninety-ninth sonnet in *Astrophel and Stella*: Sidney's conceits, mannerisms, and phrasing are everywhere in Drummond's sonnets, and it is even possible that he misremembered the word 'enamelled' from its sestet:

But when birds charm, and that sweet air which is
  Morn's messenger, with rose-enamelled skies
Calls each wight to salute the flower of bliss,
  In tombs of lids are buried then mine eyes,
    Forced by their lord, who is ashamed to find
    Such light in sense, with such a darkened mind.

Finally in this echo hunt, one might notice that the nightingale is female, something a little unexpected given that the bird and the poet are in 'like case'; this reminds the reader of the original nightingale, Philomela, in Ovid's *Metamorphoses* Book 6, who before being transformed into a bird vowed to make the forests resound with her griefs for the wrongs done to her – whence the point of the parenthesis ('so may thou Fortune milder trie'). Philomel (of either sex) is then the emblem of the grief-stricken lover forced into remote solitudes.

This sonnet, written in Sidney's favourite form, an Italian octave and an English sestet, is typical of many by Drummond

81

in having several layers of reading to offer: first, a surface texture of narrative or 'personal' utterance; behind that, the voices of other lyric poets, translated, paraphrased, or alluded to (for example, Sidney, Ronsard, Petrarch) and behind those again mythical or topos-related resonances (Ovid here), so that the myth or situation is reached through a receding series of statements of it focused in the present text. 'Who speaks here?' is a question rather hard to answer. Even granted that, before the institution of laws of copyright, the Renaissance had a much freer attitude to translation and imitation than we should think normal, Drummond's sonnet intertextualizing is still unusual.

Drummond lacked Shakespeare's metaphorical power, and he did not have Sidney's ironic and frequently deconstructive sense of humour (the wit of the phrase 'tombs of lids' in the quotation above is quite beyond him); but he does very successfully and sweetly take over Petrarch's emblematic land-scapes and his antitheses of emotions and times. Perhaps because he cannot be whimsical, he manages also a kind of quiet gravity and ceremoniousness, as in the twenty-fourth sonnet of the 1616 *Poems* (which characteristically takes off from a sonnet by the French poet Desportes, and maybe also from Shake-speare's Sonnet 22):

> In Minds pure Glasse when I my selfe behold,
> And vively see how my best Dayes are spent,
> What Clouds of Care above my Head are roll'd,
> What comming Harmes, which I can not prevent:
> My begunne Course I (wearied) doe repent,
> And would embrace what *Reason* oft hath told,
> But scarce thus thinke I, when Love hath controld
> All the best reasons Reason could invent.
> Though sure I know my Labours End is Griefe,
> The more I strive, that I the more shall pine,
> That only Death can be my last Reliefe:
> Yet when I think upon that Face divine,
> Like one with Arrow shot in Laughter's place,
> Malgre my heart I joye in my Disgrace.

vively: vividly; *controld*: checked; *Malgre*: in spite of

This is a fluent but very conservative sonnet, organized by the traditional markers of dialectic: 'when', 'but', 'though', 'yet'. The octave has a stately momentum, and the final couplet, very much in Sidney's manner, a snap and a paradox. Yet, possibly because the thought 'turns' not at the ninth line but at the seventh – in itself a good idea – one has the feeling that Drummond cannot command the linguistic or metaphorical energy of Donne or Herbert or Shakespeare to get him through the sestet, and gives a string of clichés instead. Drummond too often slides, as here, from quiet to inertness.

16

John Milton
(1608–1674)

To see this much-admired ceremoniousness at its best, we turn finally to John Milton, whose sonnet 'When I consider how my light is spent' may be one of the many echoes of Drummond in his verse. (Milton's nephew, Edward Phillips, edited Drummond's collected *Poems* in 1656.)

> When I consider how my light is spent,
>   E're half my days, in this dark world and wide,
>   And that one Talent which is death to hide,
> Lodg'd with me useless, though my Soul more bent
> To serve therewith my Maker, and present
>   My true account, least he returning chide,
>   Doth God exact day-labour, light deny'd,
> I fondly ask; But Patience to prevent
>   That murmur, soon replies, God doth not need
>   Either man's work or his own gifts, who best
>   Bear his milde yoak, they serve him best, his State
> Is Kingly. Thousands at his bidding speed
>   And post o're Land and Ocean without rest:
>   They also serve who only stand and waite.

talent: cf. Matt. 25. 14–30; *fondly*: foolishly; *gifts,*: i.e. gifts; *waite*: are in attendance

This sonnet is dominated by the master-verb 'consider': less startling and graver than Drummond's 'behold', its effect is enforced by a combination of enjambment and medial pauses (see above the comments on Herbert's sonnets), which suggest hesitation in the octave from the speaker (who is actually wiser than his own speaking self, since he calls his questions 'fond'). Then, as Patience replies, the sentences become simpler grammatically, and when the speaker is finally properly answered, the line and the thought coincide, in an epigram so famous that it has become an English proverb.

Milton was a master of the rhetorical scheme on which this sonnet turns: grammatical and syntactical suspension. By turning the normal order of words round (hyperbaton, favoured by Donne) or by inserting subclauses, he delays completing the sense. The reader has the difficulty of holding on to what has already been said while waiting for a missing item that will make full sense of it, as, for example, the verb that seems to be missing after 'my Soul more bent', and then turns out to have been simply elided: 'my Soul [is] more bent/To serve...'. And this difficulty occurs inside a huge 'when'-clause with embedded subordinate clauses winding its way down the octave, itself suspending the main verb 'ask'. Milton loved this device, and it is a feature of his epic style, as the opening lines of *Paradise Lost* show.

Both enjambments and suspensions make the reader move forward, with a sense of confronting obstacles or solving puzzles, but careful judgement is needed to avoid simply baffling the reader, as can happen, for instance, in the syntax of Gerard Manley Hopkins's lyrics. At fourteen lines, a sonnet is probably not too long to be written as a single sentence with the main verb at the end, and Sir Thomas Wyatt's 'If amours faith, an hert unfayned', for example, holds the main verb until the start of line 13. That, however, is really a list sonnet with fairly simple repetitions, and a sonnet like this, which delays the main verb while also enjambing, embedding, and disturbing normal word order, is really pushing intricacy to the limit. The most extreme instance, in Milton's twenty-four sonnets (six of which were written in Italian) is the sonnet to Sir Henry Vane, written in 1652:

> Vane, young in yeares, but in sage counsell old,
>   Then whom a better Senatour nere held
>   The helm of Rome, when gownes not armes repelld
> The feirce Epeirot and the African bold,
> Whether to settle peace, or to unfold
>   The drift of hollow states, hard to be spelld,
>   Then to advise how warr may best, upheld,
> Move by her two maine nerves, Iron and Gold
>   In all her equipage; besides to know

Both spirituall powre and civill, what each meanes,
　What severs each thou 'hast learnt, which few have don.
The bounds of either sword to thee we ow.
Therefore on thy firm hand religion leanes
　In peace, and reck'ns thee her eldest son.

then: than; *Epeirot and the African bold*: i.e. Pyrrhus and Hannibal; *spelld*: worked out

Not only is the main verb held until the eleventh line ('thou 'hast learnt'), but all its grammatical objects are subordinate clauses, which come before it in an extravagant hyperbaton – the reader simply does not know where to attach all the clauses in lines 5–11 until she or he reaches the verb. In addition, there is much compression of thought ('how warr may best, upheld . . .') and not a few Hellenisms and Latinisms ('besides to know' for 'besides knowing'). Without a knowledge of the development of the sonnet, one might uncharitably suppose that Milton's brain was so trammelled by years of writing academic and political Latin and pamphlet English that he could no longer write straight – certainly his earlier sonnets do not apply as much torque to the English language as this.

But a rereading of the sonnets of Donne and Herbert, which it is likely, though not certain, that Milton knew, suggests that he had noticed that both of these, in the service of preaching, had re-energized the language of the sonnet, Herbert by skilful enjambment and compression, and Donne by violent disturbances of word order and frequent elision of syllables. Combining these novelties, Milton produces a grave, learned, urgent, and weighty tone, very appropriate to giving civic and political advice, as he constantly did in his personal and professional life. He did indeed flirt with Petrarchan idioms in his six Italian compositions, five sonnets and one canzone stanza, written about 1629 apparently for an Italian girl named Emilia when he himself was learning Italian, but even these are much more courtly compliment and socializing than Petrarchan passion. His very first sonnet, 'O Nightingale, that on yon bloomy spray', is very like Drummond's manner, sensuous yet dignified; but after these, all his sonnets are occasional, that is, written to some specific event or social occasion, and he is the only Renaissance sonneteer to achieve high poetic standing on a handful of occasional sonnets. Such sonnets were very common, particularly as dedications or commendations in books, but the sonnet sequence, as we have seen, or the Petrarchan collection, was usually the sonnet genre to which the aspiring poet devoted his efforts.

In returning the British sonnet, at the end of its Renaissance career, to the Italian model of civic humanism, in which the poet is not a lover or a preacher, but a secular teacher of virtue, a friend and giver of good counsel, Milton was probably not aware of making a poetic statement, as he certainly thought he did in his major poems. He had visited Italy in his youth, read contemporary Italian poetry with some care, and chose to write all but four of his own sonnets in the 'Petrarchian stanza', as he called it. He certainly thought sufficiently well of his sonnets to collect and publish most of them in his last volume of poems, his *Poems etc. upon Several Occasions* of 1673, but the very title conceded their relatively light weight. What gave his sonnets their high standing in the late eighteenth and nineteenth centuries was their combination of grave moralizing, conviviality, and passion in noble causes (mostly) with their being written by the author of *Paradise Lost*, whose lightest word or most trivial piece acquired glory by association.

'The thing became a trumpet in his hands', said Wordsworth of Milton's use of the sonnet; and if today we might think some of his sonnets rather more domestic music, there is no doubt that he is unlike nearly all the other poets mentioned in this book, and in some ways very like Dante and Petrarch, Pietro Bembo (1470–1547), and particularly Giovanni della Casa (1503–1556), whose poems he owned, when these poets are writing not about Love but about other human affairs. The civic persona that these poets developed allowed them to dispense general moral advice and also specific political advice as to equals: here is Milton addressing Cromwell:

> *Cromwell*, our cheif of men, who through a cloud
>   Not of warr onely, but detractions rude,
>   Guided by faith and matchless Fortitude
> To peace and truth thy glorious way hast plough'd,
> And on the neck of crowned Fortune proud
>   Hast reard Gods trophies, and his work pursu'd,
>   While Darwen stream with blood of Scotts imbru'd,
> And *Dunbarr feild* resounds thy praises loud,
> And Worsters laureat wreath; yet much remains

To conquer still; peace hath her victories
No less renownd then warr, new foes arise
Threatning to bind our soules with secular chaines:
Helpe us to save free Conscience from the paw
Of hireling wolves whose Gospell is their maw.

rude: vulgar; *Dunbarr feild*: B. of Dunbar, 1650; *Worsters*: B. of Worcester, 1651; *maw*: gullet

This is a superb sonnet, in all senses of the word: after a huge and elaborate, though in no way fawning, compliment to Cromwell, Milton offers not a plea for favour, but an admonition, couched in a mixture of generality and aphorism, that Cromwell should not rest upon his laurels, and the closing couplet (Milton wrote only one English sonnet with a final couplet) suggests tactfully that Cromwell is only *primus inter pares*, helping in a communal enterprise. This is the voice of civic humanism: by comparison, Shakespeare is obsequious to his addressees, and Donne likewise obsequious before his God (I use the word as near as possible without pejorative implication). The Petrarchan sonnet focuses upon the internal oscillations of feeling in the speaker; the Miltonic sonnet looks outwards to the life of the body politic, and, even when Milton writes of his own condition, as in the sonnet 'To Mr Cyriack Skinner, upon his blindness' (1654), he still refers outwards to the world about him.

It is not, of course, the fact that he is writing a sonnet that makes him do this: it is the coincidence of his own independent temperament and a new emerging social and religious order. Still, the much more fluent, forward-moving sonnet developed by Herbert and Donne, and Milton's own reading of Italian sixteenth-century political and religious sonnets of similar sophistication, must have shown him how to express his temperament and his social vision. The kind of sensuous amplification and Baroque richness that attracted Drummond, and that make his sonnets melodious and decorative, Milton also responded to in his youth, as is shown by his lines 'On the Death of a fair Infant dying of a cough' (1625); but his sonnets have little of that.

And yet his last sonnet of all – and therefore probably the last British sonnet of the seventeenth century, provoked by who knows what private anguish for the death of his second wife, Catherine Woodcock, in 1658 – returns in its way to the

Petrarchan mode he had dallied with in his youth, and to the motif of the return of the beloved in a vision after her death, made famous by Dante and by Petrarch at the beginning of the sonnet's career, and used by many Italian poets (Milton may have been imitating a sonnet by Bernardino Rota (1508–75), a Neapolitan with a high reputation as the poet of conjugal love). By that time he had written all or most of *Paradise Lost*, and, like Spenser, brought to the very small area of the sonnet the skill and the effortless control acquired in the huge sounding spaces of the epic. Probably, too, there was in his head some of the undoubtedly skilled elegiac music of Drummond, whose collected poems his nephew had published two years before (1656), and he pays him the tribute of lifting, and transforming, a line (from Drummond's sonnet 'Sith it hath pleas'd that First and onlie Faire'):

> Methought I saw my late espoused Saint
>> Brought to me like *Alcestis* from the grave,
>> Whom *Joves* great Son to her glad husband gave,
> Rescu'd from death by force though pale and faint.
> Mine as whom wash't from spot of child-bed taint
>> Purification in the old Law did save,
>> And such, as yet once more I trust to have
> Full sight of her in Heaven without restraint,
> Came vested all in white, pure as her mind:
>> Her face was vail'd, yet to my fancied sight
> Love, sweetness, goodness in her person shin'd
>> So clear, as in no face with more delight.
> But O as to embrace me she enclin'd
> I wak'd, she fled, and day brought back my night.*

Son: i.e. Hercules; *fancied*: dreaming

[*Anyone whose ears are accustomed to the couplet ending of the English sonnet will hear another, and very relevant, rhyme word here.]

With the falling silent of this tough, severe, slightly pedantic, but miraculously tender voice, the sonnet too falls out of sight for a century – it was exactly 100 years after the composition of this sonnet that a minor eighteenth-century poet, Thomas Edwards, helped to revive Romantic interest in it by publishing a collection of Miltonic praise sonnets, appended to *The Canons of Criticism*, (1758). Milton's high reputation in the second half of the eighteenth century carried his sonnets with it, and his known competence in, and knowledge of, Italian language and literature, together with his admiration for Spenser, produced a kind of pedigree for Romantic writers – as late as 1892, in his learned and very readable edition of Milton's *Sonnets,* Mark Pattison sees the line as running from Dante and Petrarch to Surrey, Drummond, and Milton, with Shakespeare's *Sonnets* as a laboured and obscure collection to be critically stepped over. For a short time, indeed, at the beginning of the nineteenth century, the word 'legitimate' was used to identify the Petrarchan or Italian form of the sonnet as against the Shakespearean.

The really massive amount of sonnet writing, in all forms, in Britain and America during the nineteenth century (to speak only of sonnets in English) produced a fatigue in the early twentieth century among modernist poets; but, as a new millennium starts, the sonnet seems still to be popular not just in English but in most major languages – including, I am told, Chinese and Russian. Most influential poets writing in English have used the form, even e.e. cummings; and some, like John Berryman, have written very considerable sequences. All sorts of formal experiments have been tried, and notably among living poets Tony Harrison has developed the form and the notion of sequence in his 'from The School of Eloquence' as published in his in *Selected Poems* in 1984. Magazines that publish poetry regularly print sonnets – Elizabeth Jennings, for example, has been a contributor of many fine sonnets. So recognizable is the form, indeed, that sonnets can even be written pictorially, though that is not a modern invention: there are rebus sonnets in the sixteenth century.

Donne's invitation to 'build in sonnets pretty rooms' is still being enthusiastically accepted, and if the rooms are not always pretty they are of necessity always small and neat, though the furniture may at times be oddly arranged. The reader who wishes to study the sonnet further will find that, though the critical literature is not extensive, and, as in chess (to change the metaphor from furnishing to games), the basic rules can be learnt very quickly, and have remained the same for centuries, yet the number of games is infinite. And though this book deals only with the early British sonnet, the sonnet thrives in all European languages, and all speakers of these have a share in its international intertextuality.

17

The Sonnet and its Criticism

The criticism of the sonnet to which the reader might turn for further study is at once scanty and miscellaneous. There are very few books devoted entirely to the sonnet form, and such literary criticism of the sonnet as we have tends to occur in studies or editions of the work of an author who happened to write sonnets among his or her other poems, or as part of an introduction to an anthology of sonnets. Herbert S. Donow, *The Sonnet in England and America: A Bibliography of Criticism* (Westport, Conn., and London, 1982), gives a list of all articles and critical works up to its publication, and the thinness of the material in his 'General Criticism' section exhibits the problem.

As the Italians invented the sonnet, they also began criticism of it, and the earliest work we have is a fourteenth-century account of all the current poetic forms in vernacular verse: Antonio da Tempo, *Summa artis rithimici vulgaris dictaminis*, edited by R. Andrews (Bologna, 1977). Da Tempo's 'Brief Guide to Italian Verse-writing' lists and exemplifies all the sonnet variants known to him. This cataloguing approach was much expanded at the end of the nineteenth century (when for political and nationalist reasons it was important for Italians to establish their primacy in the sonnet) by Leandro Biadene, *Morfologia del sonetto nei secoli XIII–XIV* ('Morphology of the Sonnet in the 13th and 14th centuries') Florence, 1888; ed. and reprinted by R. Fedi, Bologna, 1977). For the English reader interested in this early period, there are two articles by the great Petrarch scholar Ernest H. Wilkins, 'The Invention of the Sonnet', *Modern Philology*, 13 (1915), 463–94, and, for the diffusion of the sonnet, 'A General Survey of Renaissance Petrarchanism', *Comparative Literature*, 2 (1950), 327–42. These are all studies that inform the reader what is there and where it occurs, rather than offering criticism. More critical, but limited to the very early period, is Christopher Kleinhenz', *The Early Italian Sonnet: The First Century, 1220–1321* (Lecce, 1986).

As the sonnet proceeded into the fifteenth and sixteenth centuries, the sonnet, up to whatever point it had reached, was often mentioned in more general treatments of the art of poetry, and a good collection of these comments, accessible through the entry 'Sonnet' in the index, is Bernard Weinberg, *A History of Literary Criticism in the Italian Renaissance*, 2 vols. (Chicago, 1961). Where such criticism is evaluative, it is usually concerned with the rhetorical scope of the sonnet: given its very small size, what kind of subjects can it handle, and with what sort of power? This issue has persisted in sonnet criticism ever since, as, for example, in William Wordsworth's sonnet, 'Scorn not the Sonnet, critic!' (1827).

British rhetorical critics in the sixteenth century, however, said almost nothing about the sonnet, despite its enormous popularity; when it was referred to, it was simply recognized as one of the small forms suitable for love poetry, with the endorsement of Petrarch, and those sonnet-writers of the time who speak about the function of the sonnet in their sonnets say no more than that. They accepted, too, the standard form of the sonnet, and showed no interest in the extended, curtailed, or specially intricate variants used in Italian writing. Even Milton, who probably had a better knowledge of Italian sonnets than his predecessors in English, left no critical comments on the form.

When in the nineteenth century the sonnet in English returned to popularity both in Britain and America, the Italian origins of the sonnet and its use in Britain by the writers of the sixteenth and seventeenth centuries were largely unknown to the literary public (the work of Sidney, Spenser, Shakespeare, and Milton excepted). Much of the theoretical writing on the sonnet therefore came in prefaces or notes to anthologies or editions, as, for example, David Main's *A Treasury of English Sonnets* (New York, 1881), and Mark Pattison's introduction to his *Milton's Sonnets* (London, 1892). This material was usually written in a spirit of informativeness, whether historical or national, rather than in a critical manner as we should think of criticism today; but nineteenth-century authors read very widely in many languages, and it would be a very well-informed modern reader who found no new material in, say, Capel Loftt's *Laura, or an Anthology of Sonnets and Elegiac Quatorzains*, 5 vols. (London, 1814). One extended study, written out of great partiality to 'the regular or legitimate Italian sonnet', is Charles Tomlinson, *The Sonnet: Its Origin, Structure and Place in Poetry* (London, 1874), but this is concerned mainly with effective translation of Italian sonnets into English; more up to date, and demonstrative of the huge interest in the sonnet in America, is the anthology, with critical essays, by Leigh Hunt and Samuel Lee, *The Book of the Sonnet*, 2 vols. (London and Boston, 1867). Milton's great prestige in the nineteenth century gave status to the Italian sonnet form that he had used, and made it popular with British and American poets, whether translating or composing their own. One of the most popular anthologies of the sonnet was also part of this Italian rehabilitation, Dante Gabriel Rossetti's *Dante and his Circle: With the Italian Poets Preceding Him (1100–1200–1300). A Collection of Lyrics Edited and Translated in the Original Metres* (London, 1874). Rossetti did not intend this as a study of the sonnet, but as an anthology of early Italian lyric poetry that also offered a translation of Dante's *Vita nuova*; he has very little to say about the sonnet form, but, as most of the lyrics in the book are sonnets, and as the collection was extremely popular (it can still be found in second-hand bookshops, and most major libraries have a copy), it diffused an awareness of the sonnet, and its reputation by association with Dante.

If this fashionable interest in Italian verse seems to have little to do with the sonnet in English, the reader should be aware that parallel, as it were, to the kind of studies mentioned above, were the series of scholarly editions of British poets, major and minor, of the Renaissance period being produced by the scholarly and antiquarian societies of the Victorian age – the Hunterian Club, the Maitland Club, the Scottish and Early English Text Societies, among others. These were not specially concerned with the sonnet form, but their labours made it possible for anyone interested in the British sonneteers of the period 1525–1670 to find reliable and informative texts. As a direct result of the work of Professor Edward Arber (1836–1912), who published many little-known sonnets and sonnet sequences in *Arber's English Reprints* (1868–71) and *A English Garner* (1877–90), there appeared in 1904 the first really good collection of sonnet sequences from our period, Sidney Lee's *Elizabethan Sonnets*, 2 vols. (Westminster, 1904). This reprinted seventeen of the major and minor sonnet sequences of the period, with an excellent historical and formal introduction of some hundred pages. It should be mentioned here that, in 1984, Holger Klein published a facsimile edition of most of the sonnet sequences that Lee had omitted, *English and Scottish Sonnet Sequences of the Renaissance*, 2 vols. (Hildesheim, 1984); so that a library that has these two texts will have a good working collection of nearly all of the British Renaissance sequences (Shakespeare and Donne excepted). It is Lee who first drew attention to the role of the musical madrigal in popularizing the sonnet, a topic that still awaits a comprehensive study, but that is of more interest to students of the French and Italian sonnet. The number of sonnets with settings in British Renaissance madrigal and lute-song books is tiny, as is shown in E. H. Fellowes, *English Madrigal Verse, 1588–1632* (Oxford, 1920).

In writing about what another anthologizer, William Sharp, called 'the sonnet, its characteristics and history' (*Sonnets of this Century* (London, n.d.[c.1885?])), the editors mentioned were going over much the same ground, Italian or British or both. The formal features of the sonnet were clear and could be briefly described, and its origins and development in Britain were also known and reviewable in published scholarly editions. What was being done for British poets was also being done for French and Italian poets by their respective scholars and publishers, and the nineteenth century ended with a very thorough and still most useful bibliographic account of the French and Italian sonnets, Hugues Vaganay, *Le Sonnet en Italie et en France au XVIme siècle* (Lyons, 1902, repr. Geneva, 1966).

The indebtedness of the British Renaissance sonnet to the French sonnet, largely ignored in the nineteenth century, was examined by Sidney Lee in the anthology referred to above, and later by two still very useful separate studies, Janet G . Scott, *les Sonnets élisabéthains* (Paris, 1929), and Lisle Cecil John, *Elizabethan Sonnet Sequences* (New York, 1938). From then until the end of the twentieth century, there was very little general discussion of the sonnet form in the Renaissance period, other than as part of the criticism of the sonnet writing of individual authors (see Bibliography). In 1955 appeared Walter Monch, *Das Sonett: Gestalt und Geschichte* (Heidelberg, 1955), which concentrated on the English and French sonnet, but pulled together in one volume most of what was known and accepted about the sonnet form and its development. It has not been translated into English. Among the few general studies in English where the reader will find excellent discussion of the Renaissance sonnet are Leonard Forster, *The Icy Fire: Studies in European Petrarchism* (Cambridge, 1969) – though, as his title suggests, Forster's main concern is elsewhere than with the sonnet form; and J. W. Lever, *The Elizabethan Love Sonnet* (London, 1956), a student mainstay for years, though working with a set of critical assumptions now outdated. One of the best general introductions to the sonnet form, lightly written, witty, and wide-ranging, but confined to Italian literature and language, was provided by G. Getto and E Sanguinetti in their anthology *Il Sonetto* (Milan, 1957).

John Fuller's short guide, *The Sonnet* (London, 1972), ranges wider than the British Renaissance sonnet, but is still the best short guide to the form. Brief also, but very useful, is the introduction to John Hale, *Sonnets of Four Centuries, 1500–1900* (Otago Studies in English, Dunedin, NZ, 1992), and the pages in Alistair Fowler's *Kinds of Literature* (Oxford, 1982) that deal with the Renaissance sonnet are theoretically invaluable, alerting the reader, as does Leonard Forster, to the connection of the sonnet, in the Renaissance rhetorical view, with the epigram, a kind of poem that Romantic literary theory has almost entirely removed from our consciousness.

It was partly because the critical material above is heterogeneous and often inaccessible to the ordinary reader that I produced my own general historical and critical study, *The Development of the Sonnet* (London and New York, 1992), taking the sonnet from its origins in Italy to the death of Milton. In addition to reviewing the various forms of the sonnet and giving an account of its development, I suggested reasons for its longlasting appeal, and proposed that its internal dynamics were uniquely appropriate to certain kinds of self-expression in lyric.

My study of the sonnet sequence, *The Sonnet Sequence: A Study of its Strategies* (New York, 1997), was more purely generic, attempting (for the first time) to define the parameters of the sonnet sequence, and it examined a range of sequences from Dante's time to the present day, including but not confined to the Renaissance sonnet sequence.

The late-nineteenth-century view of the sonnet as a lyrical vehicle for lofty thoughts, and its concerns with the expressiveness of the Italian form as against the English or Shakespearean form, often seem critically unsatisfactory now because of the theoretical problem of attaching emotional value to specific patterns of sonnet. I have myself, for example, tried to connect the final couplet of the English sonnet with prudence and worldly wisdom, but am aware that this is critically shaky; and that I am not thereby advancing very much beyond what Italian Renaissance critics had to say about gravity and wit in the sonnet. Scholarly editions of sonnets made it possible for critics in the early twentieth century to trace borrowings among sonneteers, and critics and editors then became occupied with the problem of originality: L. E. Kastner in his superb edition of *The Poetical Works of William Drummond of Hawthornden*, 2 vols. (Manchester, 1913) felt obliged to spend an enormous amount of time and space detailing all of Drummond's borrowings, but he prudently refrained from saying what should be done with this information. One may doubt whether the poststructuralist idea of intertextuality has done more than just reconceptualize this problem, as part of the postmodernist interest in the sonnet as a mode of constructing the self – with whatever problematics that word brings in its wake. Curiously, this seems to be also a return to earlier Renaissance (mainly Italian) preoccupations with the sonnet as a persuasive construct, a self-accounting designed to satisfy or convince the beloved. I do think (as I have argued it myself) that the idea of the sonnet as a problem-solving area, in which a dialectical structure brings undisciplined feelings under quite specific kinds of rhetorical control, is a most useful one, but have to admit that this is implicit much earlier in Renaissance discussions of 'passionate' verse forms.

Meantime, practising poets, largely innocent of these academic gyrations, continue to write sonnets, and readers read them, and probably also write them, because, as Don Paterson says in his millennial anthology, *101 Sonnets from Shakespeare to Heaney* (London, 1999), 'it's a box for their dreams'.

Notes

INTRODUCTION

1. Don Paterson (ed.), *101 Sonnets from Shakespeare to Heaney* (London: Faber & Faber, 1999).
2. Ibid., p. x.

SECTION 4. SIR THOMAS WYATT

1. See Michael R. G. Spiller, *The Development of the Sonnet* (London and New York: Routledge, 1992), ch. 5.

SECTION 6. ANNE LOCKE

1. George Puttenham, *The Arte of English Poesie* (London: Richard Field, 1589), ch. 31; repr. in G. Gregory Smith (ed.), *Elizabethan Critical Essays* (Oxford: Clarendon Press, 1904), ii. 62–3.

SECTION 7. SIR PHILIP SIDNEY

1. See Sidney Lee, *The French Renaissance in England* (Oxford: Clarendon Press, 1910), bk. IV.

SECTION 11. WILLIAM SHAKESPEARE

1. Katherine Duncan-Jones, 'Introduction', in *Shakespeare's Sonnets*, ed. Katherine Duncan-Jones (The Arden Shakespeare, 3rd series; Thomas Nelson & Sons, 1997), 57.
2. Rosalie Colie, *Shakespeare's Living Art* (Princeton: Princeton University Press, 1974), 72.

Select Bibliography

GENERAL WORKS ON THE SONNET AND BRITISH RENAISSANCE POETRY (INCLUDING ANTHOLOGIES)

Biadene, Leandro, *Morfologia del Sonetto nei Secoli XIII-XIV* (Florence: Le Lettre [1888]; ed. and repr. R. Fedi, Bologna, 1977). A specialist's book, but short; usefully identifies and exemplifies nearly all known Italian sonnet variants in its period.

da Tempo, Antonio, *Summa artis rithimici vulgaris* [*c*.1320], ed. R. Andrews (Bologna: Commissioni per i testi di lingua, 1977). A historical curiosity: the first description at any length of the sonnet and its variants by a critic, and one who was a contemporary of Dante and his circle.

Donow, Herbert S., *The Sonnet in England and America: A Bibliography of Criticism* (London and Westport, Conn.: Greenwood, 1982). An excellent checklist of criticism, arranged by sonneteer. It does not list editions.

Dubrow, Heather, *Echoes of Desire: Petrarchism and its Counter-Discourse* (Ithaca, NY, and London: Cornell University Press, 1995). For those who have a grasp of Petrarchism, this is a fine study of its complications and modifications in Renaissance poetry. No bibliography, but the copious footnotes are in effect a bibliography of modern criticism.

Fellowes, Edmund H., *English Madrigal Verse, 1588–1632* (Oxford: Clarendon Press, 1920). Included here because of its negative evidence, that the British song-book compilers of the period made very little use of sonnets, unlike their European contemporaries.

Ferry, Anne, *The 'Inward' Language: Sonnets of Wyatt, Sidney, Shakespeare, Donne* (Chicago: University of Chicago Press, 1983). One of the best of the many critical texts that followed Greenblatt, examining the construction of self in sonnet writing.

Forster, Leonard, *The Icy Fire: Five Studies in European Petrarchism*

(Cambridge: Cambridge University Press, 1969). Still the best short introduction to European Petrarchism: essays 1, 2, and 4 can be read as a single text.

Fowler, Alastair, *Kinds of Literature* (Oxford: Clarendon Press, 1982). Apart from its value as a seminal modern study of genres in literature, this has much to say about the connections between the sonnet and the epigram, a topic much more important in the Renaissance than it has seemed to be today.

Fuller, John, *The Sonnet* (London: Methuen Critical Idiom, 1972). A book for the hip pocket, it covers an amazing amount of ground, and in fifty pages alerts the reader to almost everything needful about the sonnet. Its bibliography is, inevitably, well out of date.

Going, William T., *Scanty Plot of Ground* (The Hague: Mouton, 1976). Though not strictly relevant to this book, this is the best single study of the English sonnet sequence in the nineteenth century, and has a crisp introduction on the connections between Renaissance sonnet writing and Romantic writing.

Greenblatt, Stephen, *Renaissance Self-Fashioning* (Chicago: University of Chicago Press, 1980) A primary text in modern Renaissance criticism, it examines how Renaissance literature handles identity and the self.

Hale, John (ed.), *Sonnets of Four Centuries, 1500–1900* (Otago Studies in English; Dunedin, NZ, 1992). One of the few modern anthologies of the sonnet for students, and one produced outside the Eurocentric literary area, with a clear and stimulating introduction.

Hunt, Leigh and Lee, Samuel, *The Book of the Sonnet*, 2 vols. (London: Sampson, Low, Son & Marston; Boston: Roberts Brothers, 1867). A large anthology incorporating essays by Hunt (d. 1859) and Lee, reminding one of the great interest in and massive production of sonnets in America.

John, Lisle Cecil, *The Elizabethan Sonnet Sequences* (New York: Columbia University, 1938). An older study, which investigates the motifs running through Elizabethan and Jacobean sonnet sequences, and does it so well that it is still referred to.

Klein, Holger (ed.), *English and Scottish Sonnet Sequences of the Renaissance*, 2 vols. (Hildesheim: Georg Olms, 1984). Noting the excellence of Sidney Lee's *Elizabethan Sonnets* (see below), Klein provides a facsimile reprint of almost all the British sonnet sequences that Lee missed, which includes the Scottish writers around James VI and I.

Kleinhenz, Christopher, *The Early Italian Sonnet: The First Century, 1220– 1321* (Lecce: Millella [1986]). Specialized and mainly for the student of Italian, it is one of the very few studies of the Italian sonnet before Petrarch accessible to the British reader.

Lee, Sidney (ed.), *Elizabethan Sonnets*, 2 vols. (Westminster [London]: Archibald Constable & Co., Ltd., 1904). Taking it as his brief to 'illustrate the close dependence of the Elizabethan sonnet on foreign models', Lee provides a still excellent critical introduction followed by reprints of the main Elizabethan sonnet sequences, excluding Shakespeare and Donne. See also under 'Klein, Holger'.

Lever, J. W., *The Elizabethan Love Sonnet* (London: Methuen, 1956). A very student-friendly account of Elizabethan sonnet writing, though the criticism takes a Romantic and confessional approach to poetry.

Loftt, Capel, *Laura, or an Anthology of Sonnets and Elegiac Quatorzains*, 5 vols. (London: B. and R. Crosby, 1814). The distinctively named Capel Loftt (whose son had the same name), lawyer, minor politician, and man of letters, furnishes evidence of the interest of English Romanticism in the European sonnet.

Main, David (ed.), *A Treasury of English Sonnets* (Manchester: Ireland & Co., 1880; Edinburgh and London: W. Blackwood & Sons, 1880; New York: R. Worthington, 1881). Reprinting nearly 500 sonnets with notes, this is good evidence of English and American late-nineteenth-century taste in sonnet writing.

Martines, Lauro, *Society and History in English Renaissance Verse* (Oxford: Basil Blackwell, 1985). A splendid introduction to how to connect poetry to the social order it inhabits: neither history nor 'literary criticism', but a stimulating combination.

Monch, Walter, *Das Sonett: Gestalt und Geschichte* (Heidelberg: F. H. Kerle, 1955). As the sonnet arrived in Germany too late (1616) to influence British writers, there is a notable absence of German criticism in this present bibliography. Monch's excellent account was unfortunately not translated into English, and is now critically dated, though well worth referring to.

Paterson, Don (ed.), *101 Sonnets from Shakespeare to Heaney* (London: Faber & Faber, 1999). As reading sonnets is the best way to study them, Faber & Faber has done a service by publishing this miscellany of sonnets, in no particular order, with surprises and new forms of sonnet on every page. Excellent for beginners, who will like the aggressive and eccentric introduction.

Pattison, Mark (ed.), *Milton's Sonnets* (London: Kegan Paul, Trench, Trübner & Co. Ltd., 1892). Still a very usable edition of Milton's work, this is interesting for its overview of British sonnet writing up to Milton.

Roche, Thomas P., *Petrarch and the English Sonnet Sequences* (New York: AMS Press, 1989). Focuses Forster's material on the English sonnet-writers, showing how they handled the material and adapted it.

Rossetti, Dante Gabriel, *Dante and his Circle: With the Italian Poets Preceding Him (1100–1200–1300). A Collection of Lyrics, Edited and Translated in the Original Metres* (London: Ellis & White, 1874). Still well worth reading, this anthology of translations of early Italian sonnets and other works by Dante and his contemporaries was very popular, and influential in establishing an image of Dante's age in British literary culture. It does not provide the Italian texts, but there is a first line Italian/English index.

Scott, Janet G., *Les Sonnets Elisabéthains* (Paris: Honoré Champion, 1929). Scott investigated English borrowings from French sonnets, and like John (see above) did it so well that it remains a standard text.

Spiller, Michael R. G., *The Development of the Sonnet* (London and New York: Routledge, 1992). The most recent attempt to trace the sonnet as a genre from its beginnings up to Milton. The emphasis is on British Renaissance sonnets, but the book has the only recent account of the development of the Italian sonnet, suitable for students with no knowledge of the language.

—— *The Sonnet Sequence: A Study of its Strategies* (New York: Twayne Publishers, 1997). A generic account of the sonnet sequence from thirteenth-century Italy to the present day, with an attempt to classify kinds of sequence.

Tomlinson, Charles, *The Sonnet: Its Origin, Structure and Place in Poetry* (London: John Murray, 1874). A critical account of the sonnet, this is biased towards the problems of translation from Italian. Its historical information is accurate within the limitations of nineteenth-century scholarship.

Vaganay, Hugues, *Le Sonnet en Italie et en France au XVIe siècle* (Lyons: au siège des Facultés Catholiques, 1902; repr. Geneva: Slatkine, 1966). Not of direct relevance to this study, but indispensable for relating the editions of French and Italian sonneteers to British production.

Waller, Gary, *English Poetry of the Sixteenth Century* (London and New York: Macmillan, 1986). While not specifically on the sonnet, this is an excellent account of the poetic concerns of the time using modern critical ideas.

Weinberg, Bernard, *A History of Literary Criticism in the Italian Renaissance*, 2 vols. (Chicago: University of Chicago Press, 1961). Embedded in this huge and very specialized survey are a large number of critical observations on the sonnet, given both in English and Italian. See under 'Sonnet' in his index.

Wilkins, E. H., 'The Invention of the Sonnet', *Modern Philology*, 13 (1915), 46394.

—— 'A General Survey of Renaissance Petrarchanism', *Comparative Literature*, 2 (1950), 327–42. Two very informative articles from the doyen of Petrarchan studies in the early 20th century.

Wilson, Katharina (ed.), *Women Writers of the Renaissance* (Athens, Ga.: University of Georgia Press, 1987). Not specifically about sonnets, but, given that there are two women writers mentioned in this study, the reader might refer to this collection of essays sympathetic to the problems of reading and understanding literature by Renaissance women.

PARTICULAR BIBLIOGRAPHY

The Encyclopedia of the Renaissance, ed. Paul F. Grendler (New York: Charles Scribner's Sons, 1999), has entries on 'The English Sonnet' and each poet mentioned.

Dante Alighieri

La Vita Nuova, ed. and tr. D. S. Servigni and E. Vasta (Chicago: University of Notre Dame, 1998). The Italian text with translation.

Petrarch, Francis

Petrarch's Lyric Poems, ed. and tr. Robert Durling (Cambridge, Mass.: Harvard University Press, 1976). The Italian text of the *Rime* with clear and accurate prose translations and a very good introduction.
Foster, Kenelm, *Petrarch: Poet and Humanist* (Edinburgh: Edinburgh University Press, 1984).

Wyatt, Sir Thomas

Collected Poems, ed. Kenneth Muir and Patricia Thomson (Liverpool: Liverpool University Press, 1969). Kenneth Muir had produced earlier a small *Collected Poems* (Muses' Library; London: Routledge, 1949), which is still an excellent working edition.
Thomson, Patricia, *Sir Thomas Wyatt and his Background* (London: Routledge & Kegan Paul, 1964).

Surrey, Henry Howard, Earl of

The Poems of Henry Howard, Earl of Surrey, ed. F. M. Padelford (Seattle: University of Washington, 1928; repr. New York, 1966). The standard scholarly edition.
Keene, Dennis (ed.), *Henry Howard, Earl of Surrey: Selected Poems* (Manchester: Carcanet Press, 1985). Not complete, but a useful pocket edition with a short biography.

Locke, Anne

A Meditation of a Penitent Sinner: Anne Locke's Sonnet Sequence, ed. K. Morin-Parsons (Waterloo, Ont.: North Waterloo Academic Press,

1997).

Collected Works, ed. Susan Felch (Renaissance English Text Society; Arizona: University of Arizona, 1999).

Spiller, Michael, 'A Literary "First": The Sonnet Sequence of Anne Locke', *Renaissance Studies* (Mar. 1997), 41–55.

Sidney, Sir Philip

The Poems of Sir Philip Sidney, ed. W. A. Ringler (Oxford: Clarendon Press, 1962). The standard edition of Sidney's poems, it has an immensely informative introduction.

Hamilton, A. C., *Sir Philip Sidney: A Study of his Life and Works* (New York and London: Cambridge University Press, 1977).

Waller, G., and Moore, M. (eds.), *Sir Philip Sidney and the Interpretation of Renaissance Culture* (London: Croom Helm, 1984). Useful not only for the reading of Sidney, but also for ways to read the poetry of his age.

Daniel, Samuel

Poems and a Defence of Rhyme, ed. A. C. Sprague (Cambridge, Mass.: Harvard Univesity Press, 1930; repr. 1950, 1965). Though now sixty years old, this edition is compact, scholarly, and pleasant to read.

Rees, Joan, *Samuel Daniel: A Critical and Biographical Study* (Liverpool: Liverpool University Press, 1964). A clear, sensible, and informative account.

Svensson, Lars-Håkan, *Silent Art: Rhetorical and Thematic Patterns in Samuel Daniel's* Delia (Lund: CWK Gleerup, 1980). A hugely detailed reading of *Delia*, valuable less for its theories of structure than for the enormous diligence with which Svensson has traced Daniel's sources, references, and allusions.

Spenser, Edmund

Spenser's Minor Poems, ed. E. de Selincourt (Oxford: Oxford University Press, 1910). Not a very informative introduction, but a clear and accurate scholarly text.

Shire, Helena, *A Preface to Spenser* (London and New York: Longmans, 1978). Spenser's sonnets are completely overshadowed in criticism by *The Faerie Queene*, but Mrs Shire's volume is a good place to start.

Drayton, Michael

The Works of Michael Drayton, ed. J. W. Hebel, K. Tillotson, and B. H. Newdigate, 5 vols. (Oxford: Oxford University Press, 1931–41). Because Drayton reprinted and revised his sonnets over a long period, it is useful to have a full edition to consult. A corrected edition was published in 1961 (Oxford: Basil Blackwell).

Brink, Jean R., *Michael Drayton Revisited* (Boston: Twayne Publishers, 1990).

Shakespeare, William

The editions and the critical literature on Shakespeare's *Sonnets* are so vast in quantity and variable in quality that the reader is advised to consult, in the first instance, the bibliographies of a few reputable modern editions. Three are suggested below, together with one or two major critical works that reflect modern concerns with Shakespeare's art.

Shakespeare's Sonnets, ed. W. G. Ingram and Theodore Redpath (London: Hodder & Stoughton, 1964; 3rd impression, 1978). For clarity, good sense, and modesty, this edition is a delight to use, though it lacks a critical and biographical introduction.

The Sonnets, ed. G. Blakemore Evans (The New Cambridge Shakespeare; Cambridge: Cambridge University Press, 1996). This edition places all its notes (other than variants) and commentary at the end, thus giving the student the chance to read 'straight through' if desired. A short critical introduction and a useful reading list.

Shakespeare's Sonnets, ed. Katherine Duncan-Jones (The Arden Shakespeare, 3rd series; Thomas Nelson & Sons, 1997). With a stimulating and informative introduction, a clear text (but rather cramped notes), and 'A Lover's Complaint' included, this brings the student up to date with modern scholarship. The bibliography is a bibliography of the author's references, rather than for further reading.

Fineman, Joel, *Shakespeare's Perjured Eye* (Berkeley and Los Angeles: University of California Press, 1986). The most intense modern examination of subjectivity in the *Sonnets*.

Calvert, Hugh, *Shakespeare's Sonnets and Problems of Autobiography* (Braunton [Devon]: Merlin Books, 1987). A little-known but extremely useful book, not written to scholarly standards but gathering together in one place a great deal of information about all the readings of the *Sonnets*, from the deranged to the critical mainstream.

Dubrow, Heather, *Captive Victors: Shakespeare's Narrative Poems and Sonnets* (Ithaca, NY: Cornell University Press, 1987). Pursuing a clear thesis, this is an investigation of the paradoxes of personality in Shakespeare's poetry.

Vendler, Helen, *The Art of Shakespeare's Sonnets* (Cambridge, Mass.: Harvard University Press, 1997). A luxurious and very detailed rhetorical reading of all the *Sonnets*, this is not an edition, but it does very usefully print a facsimile of each sonnet from the 1609 *Quarto* above Vendler's own edited text. The bibliography is comprehensive and up to date, and excludes the daft and trivial.

Honan, Park, *Shakespeare, a Life* (Oxford: Oxford University Press, 1998). Detailed but very readable, the most recent academic account of Shakespeare.

Donne, John

Poems, ed. H. J. C. Grierson, 2 vols. (Oxford: Oxford University Press, 1912). The standard scholarly edition, which has all the information needed to cope with the problems of dating and assembling Donne's sonnets. Its modern successor is *Donne: The Divine Poems*, ed. Helen Gardner (Oxford: Clarendon Press, 2nd edn., 1978), more compact but harder to use.

Complete English Poems, ed. C. A. Patrides (Everyman's Library; London and Melbourne: Dent, 1985). Footnoted, and with an excellent bibliography.

Bald, R. C., *John Donne: A Life* (Oxford: Clarendon Press, 1970; rev. 1986). The standard biography.

Carey, John, *John Donne: Life, Mind and Art* (London: Faber, 1981). A good biographical and critical study.

Herbert, George

The Works of George Herbert, ed. F. E. Hutchinson (Oxford: Clarendon Press, 1941; repr. 1978). The standard scholarly edition, with a useful introduction.

Summers, Joseph H., *George Herbert, his Religion and Art* (Cambridge, Mass.: Harvard University Press, 1954).

Vendler, Helen, *The Poetry of George Herbert* (Cambridge, Mass.: Harvard University Press, 1975). Since Herbert is only occasionally a sonneteer, this and the study in the previous entry incorporate discussion of his sonnets into a more general critique of his lyric poetry.

Wroth, Lady Mary

The Poems of Lady Mary Wroth, ed. Josephine A. Roberts (Baton Rouge, La., 1983). As Lady Mary Wroth is a fairly recent discovery, this is the only edition, and has an excellent introduction.

Miller, Naomi J., and Waller, Gary, *Reading Mary Wroth: Representing Alternatives in Early Modern England* (Jamaica: University of the West Indies, 1991).

Drummond of Hawthornden, William

The Poetical Works of William Drummond of Hawthornden, ed. L. E. Kastner, 2 vols. (Manchester: Manchester University Press, 1913). With modesty and erudition, Kastner did two things so well in this edition that it remains indispensable for anyone seriously interested in Drummond: he sorted out the bibliography of Drummond's works, and identified most of the borrowings in his poems.

Masson, David, *Drummond of Hawthornden: The Story of his Life and Writings* (London: Macmillan & Co., 1873). The standard life: Masson appears to have read everything and known or suspected almost everything about Drummond, and the work is written with huge quotations and an exuberantly romantic style that no academic would get away with nowadays.

Macdonald, Robert H., *The Library of Drummond of Hawthornden* (Edinburgh: Edinburgh University Press, 1971). Despite its bibliographic scope, this is a mine of information about Drummond's education and reading, something on which Masson (see above) has relatively little to say.

Jack, R. D. S., *The Italian Influence on Scottish Literature* (Edinburgh: Edinburgh University Press, 1972). Jack's fourth chapter, 'After the Union' (of the Crowns of Scotland and England in 1603), has a sympathetic and insightful account of Drummond's absorption and reworking of Italian poetry.

Milton, John

As with Shakespeare, the literature is enormous, and the sonnets themselves are dispersed through and involved in Milton's whole life. The standard edition of the poetry is *Milton's Poetical Works*, ed. Helen Darbishire, 3 vols. (Oxford: Clarendon Press, 1955). For general use, see *The Poems of John Milton*, ed. John Carey and Alastair Fowler (London and New York: Longmans, 1968; rev. 1980).

Smart, J. S., *The Sonnets of Milton* (Glasgow: Macklehose & Jackson, 1922), reissued and ed. B. A. Wright (Oxford: Clarendon Press, 1966). An excellent, fully annotated edition of the sonnets with a very good introduction on the Italian sonnet and its relevance to Milton.

Honigmann, E. A. J., *Milton's Sonnets* (London and Melbourne: Macmillan; New York: St Martin's Press, 1966). Particularly good on the dating of the sonnets.

Parker, William Riley, *Milton: A Biography*, 2 vols. (Oxford: Clarendon Press, 1968). In this really splendid biography, the sonnets are dealt with as they occur in Milton's life. Use the index.

Index of Names

[Figures in **bold type** refer to the section devoted to the author. Names of the form 'de Sade' are indexed under 'D'.]

111